The Letter Writing Project

To Bonnie,
Thank you for believing!
Love,
Wendy

THE LETTER WRITING PROJECT
Copyright © 2014 Wendy Wolff
www.wendywolff.com

Published by:
Blooming Twig Books
New York / Tulsa
www.bloomingtwig.com

All rights reserved. This book may not be photocopied for personal or professional use. No part of this book may be reproduced, stored in a retrieval system, or transmitted in any form or by any means (electronic, mechanical, photocopying, recording, or otherwise) without permission in writing from the author and/or publisher.

eBook ISBN 978-1-61343-070-5
Paperback ISBN 978-1-61343-071-2

First Edition
Printed in the United States of America.

*This book is dedicated to my sister.
May you be living in glory on the other side.
I hope our childhood dog, Pretzel Von
Schnitzel, is sitting in your lap.*

The Letter Writing Project

Wendy Wolff

*"Sister, I hear you laugh –
my heart fills full up.
Keep me please.
Sister, when you cry,
I feel your tears running down my face.
Sister, Sister keep me."*

— Dave Matthews

Table of Contents

Preface 17
    The Letter 19
    Sisters 23
    Legacy of Letter Writing 25
    The Letter Writing Project 29
    The Letter Writing Movement 31
    Letter from Donna 33

This is About You 35

ONE. Four Parts of a Broken Heart 39
    On Rage 41
    On Sorrow 45
    On Complicated Love 47
    On Condolences 51

TWO. Remorse 55
    On Being Mean 59
    On Accepting Cruelty as the Norm 63
    On Truth in Jest 67
    On Regrets 71

THREE. Love Letters 75
    On Safety 81

Letter from Donna 83
On Unconditional Love 85
On Feeling Loved 89
On Comfort 93

FOUR. Judgments 103
On Attachments 107
On the Right Thing Happening 111
On Helping Others 117
On Showing Off 121

FIVE. Heroes 125
On Amazing Adults 129
On Friendship 131
On Changing the World 133
On Being There 135
On Dedication 137
On Chance 141

SIX. Is This the Best We Can Do? 145
On Not Caring Enough 147
On Nonsense 153
On Boredom 155
On Snitching 157
On Raising Good People 159
On Providing Help 161

SEVEN. To You 165
On Next Steps 169
On Writing Letters 171

EIGHT. The Final Conversation 179
    On Being Sisters 183

About the Author 189

Acknowledgments

If my husband hadn't casually mentioned for me to do something with the letter that I wrote for my sister's memorial, this movement would have never come alive. Thank you, Marc, for giving me the space and time to create.

A mighty thanks to my youngest son whose constant excitement about this book kept me focused on finishing. His grand vision was the perfect catalyst to keep me writing. To my oldest son, I thank you for being such a good role model for me. You always have been the kindest person that I have ever known.

Many heartfelt thanks for the encouragement and assistance that I received from my mother who resides with only one daughter left in the world. Thank you for reading, praising, and proofreading every single word. To my dear confidante, Kitty your role in this process was invaluable.

Kent Gustavson with Blooming Twig Books deserves an award for being able to take my thoughts and build on them in ways that were perfectly fitting. Thank you, Kent, for making The Letter Writing Project come alive! I could never have gotten here without your brilliance.

Years back, Ana SanJuan was the first person to help me recognize my original medicine and understand how to be brave enough to share it with the world. This project is your result.

Thank you to Amy Birks, Advocate for Inspired Living, for the coaching sessions and furious commitment to my vision.

Whitney Scott's undeniable certainty about the ability of my writing to change lives kept me moving more than she knew.

Thank you to Wendy Snodgrass for using your coveted personal time to edit and provide such genuine enthusiasm.

A special thank you to every person that picks this up, passes it along, writes a letter or takes any positive action related to The Letter Writing Project. Making the world a kinder, better place is something we all share.

Preface

I will forever hear my mother's voice screaming into the phone that my sister was dead.

The sound of her voice and the finality of the words, I will always hear.

That was the day that my heart officially broke in two.

On April 2, 2011 at 4:55pm a man fell asleep as he was coming off the highway to stop at a red light. Instead of stopping, his sleeping foot was placed firmly on the gas pedal while he plowed full speed right into the driver's side of my sister's car. My sister had been waiting patiently at the red light to get on the highway. She was taking her youngest son to visit a friend. I imagine they were singing something uplifting while waiting for the light to turn green.

From across the road's divider, this man's sleeping car and slumbering foot instantaneously killed my big sister. This action eliminated a spectacular mom, wife, daughter, sister, and friend from the world. I will forever hear my mother's hysterical, earsplitting screams into the phone a few hours later that Donna was dead. My inconsolable, heartbroken mother had the appalling job of passing on the news that her beloved, special, first born miracle was gone without any notice or any way to say goodbye. My first reaction to the call was utter disbelief and so I was thrown into my usual habit of calming her down and telling her it would be okay. As those words started to come out of my mouth, the reality set in. There was no longer a Donna in the world. She was gone. We would never hear her cackle as she laughed or see her frizzy, brown mop-top again. I remember dropping to my knees in the middle of a banquet hall filled with revelers and whispered, I'm on my way.

Much later that evening, a dreaded time period arrived in which a frenzied interrogation replayed itself in my head. When was the last time I told her I loved her? Did she realize how much of my life I had focused on living up to her expectations? Did I even remember to send her that last birthday card several weeks back? When had we talked? Did she get the photo this morning that I posted for her? Why had I been so withholding of some angry feelings for weeks? Why hadn't I just talked with her?

Upon the grief, I piled layers and layers of self-hatred, anger, remorse, and shame. For days, there was brooding over the smallest of details: What about...? How come I didn't...? Why did I wait? All were valid questions without any possible solutions. That time had passed. It would never ever be regained.

The Letter

If I had only been brave enough to reveal how I had been feeling for the past few weeks prior to her death. I had been waiting to figure out the right things to say that would lend themselves to productive conversation without a huge, nasty confrontation. Finally, with pen in hand I crafted the following letter. Only it was too late. It's impossible to deliver a letter to someone who is no longer alive. As I scribbled, the words began dark, mean, and accusatory. Yet, half way through, something inside of my heart lifted and led me in a direction towards finding solace even though I have never been sadder in my life.

Dear Donna,

I want you to know that for the past few weeks I've been angry with you. While our phone conversations have been light and happy, I was not. I forced myself to pretend that I didn't take it profoundly personal that you wouldn't attend my oldest son's celebration. The words that you used that day were what hurt me the most.

You said, "I could go but I'm making the conscious choice to not go." You wanted me to clearly know that this decision was not one taken lightly and that you take responsibility for your actions. While the circumstances for your absence were all valid and true, the specific words you used made me think otherwise. The way I took it was that you were simply choosing not to come to the most important event of my child's life. In my mind I could understand that the trip was incredibly complicated and that you were being clear about your choice, but in my heart it felt like rejection. Forever and a day, I have tried to make you proud of me. This moment would have been one of those times that you could have been proud, instead you "chose" not to come.

I wish I had taken the time to tell this to you so that we could have talked it over. Maybe you would have changed your mind and come, had I not said, "I understand," when I clearly did not. I wish I had been braver. The lesson for me is to communicate the absolute truth in my heart without being afraid of the consequences. I would have done anything to learn this with you STILL HERE. Now, I'm left with this abhorrently vile taste in my mouth for MYSELF. There will always be my immeasurable regret that I lived the last 30 days of your life with unspoken hurt between us.

I love you. I miss you every minute of every day. Wishing we were laughing together on the fluffy, white couch in your den.

Love,
Wendy

So there I sat, doubled over in pain from the convulsions my body insisted on doing to manage the gobs of tears that were flowing down my face. I must have sat with pen in hand and face streaked from tears for close to an hour, which is practically impossible for me. What was I ever going to do without my sister in this world? Who will I really be now that my identity had changed from being a set of daughters to simply me? There were no answers that readily came. However, I can now assure you that time, insight, and consistent personal growth helped to heal the pain. I ended up using the long lost art of letter writing as a formal tool to uncover and clear away circumstances that were keeping me small. Letter writing allowed me to deeply feel my heartache with the intent of alleviating the sadness that led to the creation of a space in my heart for renewal.

Sisters

While my sister and I were wildly different people, we were – bottom line – sisters. As kids, I adored her and emulated her every move. She was three years older and insisted on acting like my 2nd mommy. She liked to bake chocolate cakes, so I became a trusty assistant. She liked Peter Frampton, so I listened to him regularly. She wore her hair curly, so I did the same. I continually sought her approval for things both big and small. I loved my sister so very much, even though she could be highly disapproving of me. Throughout our lives I was always afraid of disappointing her. She was a strong-willed, opinionated woman who thoroughly believed in her convictions, and that was that. This made it scary for me to show my true self for fear of her biting criticism. I was more of a free spirit who sought out the next bout of childhood hilarity, while she took on the role of caretaker regarding the way she envisioned things were supposed to be. I was smiling; she was grimacing. Much of this was not her fault, caused by an early 70's divorce of our parents and later disappearance of our father. She was a pre-teenager who was embroiled in the harsh reality of our new lives, whereas I was able to pretend that all was well in my world.

Inside and underneath it all she was simply searching for a place to belong. Her tough, prickly exterior held a more fragile, fearful person, yet I still found myself shying away from her brash sense of disapproval. She was sharp-tongued and quick to respond. I was easily offended and always defensive.

I began to share less of the beauty inside of my personal discoveries and me because I felt that they would never be accepted. Sadly, while I loved her so very much, I learned to keep potentially controversial things private. We shared so much intimacy, but it was usually over things that wouldn't displease her.

It was the act of becoming a mother that changed her in the most beautiful of ways. Finally, she belonged to something powerful and had a purpose. I felt as though being a mom was healing for her, as she was able to create emotional stability for her children that neither of us felt we had growing up. She was changing in leaps and bounds. Her harshness subsided and I felt less afraid of her judgments. As the years wore on, she continued on a quest to learn how to forgive old wounds and be full of faith. With these accomplishments, our lives as sisters took on new meanings. She taught me how to advocate for my son, be the best mother I can be, and to always find my faith. My ability to pull this book together is a direct result of her influence on my life.

As the days drew near to my sister's memorial and the crying subsided, I had brief moments when I could formulate the words that would help me honor her. I wandered aimlessly through rooms teeming with various well-wishers, wondering how I would deliver a good memoriam of my sister. Almost robotically my pen led me in the direction to what came most naturally, which was to express myself in the form of a letter.

Legacy of Letter Writing

My sister and I had always corresponded in the written form. Letters meant the world to us. My mother was a gifted letter writer, crafting a thought or two for us on small squares of white, personalized paper with the words From the Desk of... inscribed on top. We girls could regularly count on her written words whenever we were away, and most often in our plastic, I Dream of Jeannie lunchboxes. Our grandfather, owner of the 1960s Hanro Publishing Company, wrote letters to us for three decades, until his eyesight faded and his handwriting mirrored the trembling in his aging hands. His letters always started, My Darling Wendy and wrapped up with Much Love and Kisses, Your Grandpa. How I miss him.

I suppose most dramatic though, were the five or six letters we would receive over the years from our long-lost father. They would arrive with no warning and in a pale blue envelope with gracefully rounded letters taking the shape of our names. I could see my father's tobacco filled pipe resting on what I imagined his kitchen table still looked like, even though I had not seen it in five years. A red and white checked tablecloth with an overflowing, auburn glass ashtray filled with the ends of Lark cigarettes that belonged to his new wife. I envisioned a stack of hard cover, classic books like Little House on the Prairie and The Box-Car Children casually placed next to an empty box of Frosted

Flakes cereal. Her two girls, nearly our same size and shape, replaced us as his beloved daughters.

Our hands would tremble with a blend of excitement and fear as we ripped through the envelope to hear from Daddy. I can distinctly recall the tumultuous adolescent days when I would check the mailbox every single day. I was alone in my teenage misery, consistently in trouble and always misunderstood. I would open the squeaky, rust-hinged door of the black, metal mailbox bursting with hope and full of dread. Those letters meant the world to me and made me sick to my stomach. They came so infrequently and often with a hopeless, miserable, dead-end road to nowhere. Regardless of their professions of love and hope for renewal, there was never any change. The cycle of despair repeated over and over and over.

Donna and I constantly wrote to each other. Through multiple summers at separate sleep away camps, our individual college lives, our children, and our marriages, we always wrote. Sometimes her letters would come on a fancy piece of stationary with turquoise butterflies lining the margins. Other times, I'd come home to a crisp, white, business envelope with a long note written in her distinct handwriting on a yellow legal pad. As the technology age came upon us, we became slaves to the speed of email. Every day we would eagerly find five minutes to jot down the happenings of our lives with a quick burst of love received by the reader. Regardless of the medium, her letters always started with "Hi Wen" and ended with "Love, Don." That was us.

On that dreary yet sunny Saturday in April, I summoned up the courage to read my letter at the memorial service through the horror of being wholly miserable. I felt lousy and the migraine that had attacked my brain got worse with every tear I shed. My mother could barely stand up without the support of my uncle. This, in itself, was unbearable. Then add the lost faces of my nephews and my broken heart felt like it was scattered around on the floor below. My youngest son took turns rubbing my back and Grandma's. Everyone felt so miserable and helpless.

When my turn came, I read my letter to a crowd of 500 or so mourners. The response was overwhelmingly profound. People were honored to understand a primal aspect of Donna that only a sister would know. Afterwards, sisters flocked to me, pronouncing their love for each other and renewing their commitment to keep their relationship vibrant and alive. There were strangers that grabbed me and waited in line to thank me for my honesty. Some even asked for a copy of the letter. At that moment, I was just surviving, but months later, my husband murmured to me that I should 'do something with that letter.' And so I am.

The Letter Writing Project

The Letter Writing Project began as a tribute to my sister on the day that the world was remembering her, and has morphed into an activity to say the things that you need to say before it is too late. Since its inception, I wrote letters to friends, children, teachers, cousins, neighbors, and anyone I could think of. Some I mailed and some are still sitting in my "to be tossed" pile. The Letter Writing Project helped me to peel back the layers and figure out what is important in my life. I have found, through letter writing, what I love and what I don't love. Some letters I will never have any addresses for and yet I still wrote the letter. With most of my letters I eliminated the possibility that if tragedy should strike again in my life, I will never again be left with my thoughts festering inside of me. My sister died when I was a bit out of touch with her. I can never take that back.

That helpless feeling of regret will always loom over me regarding my sister, but The Letter Writing Project has prevented that from ever happening again. The letters in this book are professions of love, apology, retribution, anger, grief, remorse, joy, fulfillment, gratitude, spirituality, and hatred. They have created a space for me to further clarify exactly who I am in this world. What an enormous gift.

The Letter

This is my wish for you, the reader. Write your letters. Give yourself the reward of emotional freedom. When you craft a letter of love or admiration of someone else, imagine the joy they'll receive when they open their mailbox and find your words. Use letter writing to figure out what makes you the person that you are today. Continue to peel back the layers until you have written everything down and are left with a pure sense of self. Mail only the letters that you are proud of and that will help to make the world a better place. Don't be afraid to write the letters when there is anger festering deep inside your belly. Get all of those thoughts out of your body and then rip the paper into tiny pieces, shredding the anger into bits. You may find out that your burden has lifted and you feel lighter. You might see a few next steps to take towards healing what has been aching within your heart. It's possible that you will create a new you by developing a deeper level of personal honesty, and I find that simply incredible.

My primary rule is to never mail something that will drag a person down. Always have their highest intention in your heart. As world-renowned author, Mike Dooley, states, "thoughts become things so choose the good ones." If something still troubles you, maybe it's time to get some professional help with solving what is causing you such enormous grief.

In 2012, on the anniversary of my sister's death, my husband gave me a heartfelt present. Unbeknownst to me, he saved my sister's emails for almost twenty years. Then, exactly one year after her death, on the second saddest day of my life, he handed me a two-inch, professionally bound book of every email he could find between the two of us. After sobbing until my eyes were sore, I grabbed an icy, cold glass of water, stepped onto the back patio, and read. It took me hours to pore over every word. While the afternoon sun, turned the sky from baby blue to pinkish-orange, I reclined in the lounge chair and heard my sister's voice come alive in my head. Notes about a sick child, and recipes for her finicky set of eaters, were so amazingly joyous to read. Our common, everyday words became a precious gift. The letters immediately brought us back together, and by simply reading them I could hear her again. Amazing!

You never know if your letters might do the same for someone else one day. Below is one of my favorite passages that I received from her on January 28, 2002, the day after my husband and I arrived home from adopting our children in Russia. The email had shown up in my in-box after traveling nearly 24 hours with two toddlers. We were new parents with zero experience, about to embark on the greatest mission of our lives.

Letter from Donna

[Monday, January 28, 2002 at 7:40am]

Hi Wen,

Welcome Home! I can't wait to hear all about my little nephews. I'm so excited! I know that you guys are jet lagged and have your hands full. I'll wait for you to call me, only don't take too long. Hi Andre and Roman! It's Aunt Donna! Love ya.

This is About You

There are so many ways to use this book. Most importantly, use it as an example to understand how you feel about someone or something and then write everything that is in your heart on a piece of paper. Express your innermost sentiments. Get to know the things that you respect, value, honor, and need to change. Write letters to people whom you love and admire. Tell someone that they made a difference in your life. Use the final chapter for tips to increase your success while minimizing any stress that may occur when composing letters. Take this opportunity to change your life by eliminating stress and increasing joy.

I wish you good luck on your letter-writing endeavor. You can connect with me anytime and tell me about your letters. Join the movement to free yourself from burden and express your love for the people in your life.

    Love, Wendy
    wendy@wendywolff.com

The Letter Writing Project

Chapter One –

Four Parts of a Broken Heart

On Rage

Rage curls up and seems invisible inside of our bodies and psyche. It can remain hidden nearly forever. Some can manage to keep it suppressed for long intervals. However, when rage starts to boil it can blast its way to the surface causing insurmountable destruction as it finally finds air.

Part one of a broken heart begins with RAGE. I saw the tip of it begin to rip through me as I slumped over the dark wood pew during my sister's memorial service. At the time, I wasn't sure what it was. But I remember hearing the roar of its movement muffled with my bawling cries, showing me that if I didn't manage it, I would be in serious trouble one day.

We really had no definitive answers about why the accident occurred. All we knew was that the driver may have had a sketchy past since he fell sound asleep with his foot on the gas. As my nephew slowly healed from his internal injuries, we waited for a reason as to why my sister was dead. And so with every unanswered question my rage ball became tighter and more forceful. My sister was still gone and no one was reporting any responsibility on behalf of the driver. Poor mom still can't stomach seeing any kind of red, pick-up truck. She loses her breath and almost always lets out a small cry.

The following letter is the first one that I wrote for this book. It was the only way I could figure out how to sanely deal with letting my rage escape in a healthy manner.

> Dear Driver who killed my sister,
>
> YOU STUPID, CARELESS IDIOT!
>
> The word around town was that there were some "reasons" why you fell sound asleep coming off the highway and slammed right into my sister's car. The only item separating your speeding vehicle and your foot pressed down on the gas from my sister was a piece of metal. Do you know that when metal is hit with severe force, it crumbles like a tissue? Guess what was on the other side of that metal? My sister's body and her child!! And yes, I blame YOU.
>
> Here's the real kicker. As you know, since the authorities said you didn't have any significant amounts of substances in your system, they consider the cause of you falling asleep to simply be an accident. You are free from jail. Free from fines. Free with your life. Free.
>
> You walked away while my mother lost her daughter. The nightmare that followed for her should not have been hers to own. We will never, ever feel the warm touch of Donna's hands in ours again. Our lives will be so much less important because there is no Donna to laugh with. Instead of the tender burst of happiness that would accompany receiving her phone calls, there is a black hole of dread, since the phone will never

ring with her on the other end again.

My nephews lost their Mommy and I will never see my beloved big sister again. I can feel my anger bubbling over at times because you got to walk away – maybe even get some much needed rest, while we were left to GRIEVE this chaos. Who in the world falls asleep at the wheel? Don't you know that you should pull over if you are that tired? To me, this was no accident. It was a grown man making choices that led him to go behind the wheel and kill my sister.

I will never ever forgive you. Don't worry, I don't think about you or shoot daggers at you with my thoughts. I use my energy on better things, like worrying about my nephews, hoping they can manage to thrive without their loving, caring mom. I have emerged from the terror and trauma of the situation. My hope is that if anyone should be in this same, horrific circumstance, they will manage their rage to ward off self-destruction. And let me tell you, this was NO EASY FEAT. It has taken every skill I have to find the compassion for your poor decision-making that led to the death of my beloved sister. I miss her every moment.

Forever saddened by your actions,
Donna's little sister, Wendy

On Sorrow

I had never met sorrow in my adult life until my sister's death. There was this sense of being removed from all that once seemed normal. A passing sound, or drifting smell, could immediately propel me into agony and despair. The constricting hold over me was sorrow, and once I figured it out, I found a space in my broken heart for it to remain.

Nearly one year, almost to the day of my sister's death, another tragic loss of life occurred that rattled me to the bones. A catastrophic school bus accident claimed the life of my dear friend's youngest son. Many injuries, one death: her child. I write this letter because the pain that my beloved friend felt over the loss of her baby boy put my own pain in perspective. My friend, awaiting the return of her spunky, sweet, fabulously cheery, nine year old son from school, instead got the worst news a mother could ever receive. I could never imagine either of my beautiful boys leaving for school and not ever returning. This thought makes me gasp for air. There is no way to help except to make more room in my broken heart for my friend's sorrow. I decided to care for it like it is my own, praying that she will once again wake up to a new day, seeing that the sun still shines.

To Aaron, the boy with the bright,
brown eyes that twinkled when he smiled,

I am sure you are watching all of us now, so you know how courageous your mom, dad, and brother have been since the day you left them. Your tragic passing hit our entire community and laid a vast layer of grief among thousands of children and adults. You were loved and adored by so many people. The City police force and the Sheriff's office deputies made sure that each traffic intersection was blocked for miles to make room for the hundreds of cars in the funeral procession.

Your amazingly sweet and caring attitude was felt by so many people. Every day your mom demonstrates to me what bravery truly looks like, as she had to face an inordinate number of people that would tilt their heads with sadness and pity. Your talented and artistic dad created a peaceful sanctuary crafted out of stone with an eternal gas lantern, for people to sit and reflect about your life. Both of your parents have done their best to heal, but life will never be the same for them again. For me personally, I gained a deeper friendship with your mom that I am forever grateful for, however I would give it back in a second so that you could reappear. Rest in peace, bright-eyed angel. We all deeply miss you.

Love,
Wendy (Andre & Roman's Mom)

On Complicated Love

I consider a father to be the person who raises you. He is the guy that takes the time to care for you every day of your life. I'm lucky that a second chance was given to us when my mom got remarried, so that I could have a great father. The role of father does not necessarily belong to the man who was in your life for seven or eight years and then sporadically over the next few decades. Even if he does sign the bottom of his infrequent letters, Love Dad. "Father" is not a title given to someone who participates now and again. The father is there, always.

The third part of a broken heart is about complicated love between an absent father and a concerned daughter. Yes, I *loved* him. However, it was the memory of him that I loved and yearned for. I wanted to be with my Daddy, with the strong, piano hands making the whole house tingle with music. I wanted the light to be on in his music studio and the air to waft with the scent of his tobacco filled pipe as I ran in from the long walk home from school. I longed for the love I'd feel as I'd sit on his lap, using my fingers to trace the outline of where his glasses fell on the tip of his ear. His voice, his humming, his heartbeat; I loved them all, yet they were no longer real because they were gone. I could no longer see or feel his love. I simply remembered it. It was a complicated love and it broke my heart.

This letter has been a long time coming, and it took me years to actually have the courage to say the truth. Not the fairy-tale type of truth in which my long lost, beloved daddy comes back to be a stable support in my life. But the truth of how I really feel regarding the loss I felt after his departure before my pre-teen years, and its impact on my development. I had an amazing father who raised me, but not my daddy. My daddy left us for another woman and a new family.

Dear Daddy,

When I was five years old, you said I was your sunshine. My mother loved me, my sister played with me, and you illuminated an exuberance that equaled the rays of the sun when I was near. This all changed as quickly as a blink of an eye.

In my world as a child, I saw only good and left the unpleasantness to the adults, until that day. The day I was forced to understand issues greater than my little mind could bear. You were leaving. The man that shouted to anyone who would listen that I was his prodigy was leaving. Off to live a different life with a new family. Were we not good enough? I thought I was your sunshine? The tears I cried over the loss of you were the tears that showed me at six years old how unyielding heartbreak could be. After what seemed like days of sobbing on my mother's lap, I recall making a vow to myself to never experience that kind of loss again as long as I could help it.

Your immature narcissism to have a whimsically fulfilled life with your singer/starlet wife was at the expense of your two little daughters. You broke our hearts. We adored you. Our family was perfect according to Donna and I, and your departure severed us deeply. It took me nearly twenty years to figure out why I had been so afraid of love. Time would go by with intermittent, pain-filled visits with your daughters feeling more like outsiders in the life of their Daddy, until finally, it got so unbearable that we felt compelled to say goodbye. My loss of you taught me as a young adult that love never wins or stays around. This adopted philosophy ended up creating a series of poor decisions and inappropriate behavior on my part.

Now, with four decades gone by, and maybe a handful of interactions over the years between the two of us, I can say that I am grateful that you left. I learned an intense amount about myself though my improper, unhealthy relationships with men. Finally ending with a five-year healing process that taught me I won't actually die from a broken heart.

So much else could be said, but why waste the time? Life has been good to me. With half my life over, I am young in heart and mind. I am wise, kind, open-minded, unafraid to love, and thanks to my husband and children I get to hear the word Daddy used on a daily basis in celebration of LOVE rather than a reminder of loss.

Be well,
Wendy

On Condolences

Giving condolences is a strange concept. There were numerous faces that actually recoiled in horror when they learned of my sister's tragic death, followed by a blank stare and limited words. I saw myself actually reaching out to them with a comforting pat on the shoulder, saying it will be okay. It is here in this exact spot, where I realized the fourth part of my broken heart. Instead of receiving compassion, understanding, and sympathy, I got weird looks, timidity, and avoidance.

My dearest and closest friends found it effortless to arrange meals and sit with me as I stared into space – which I found so nourishing. However, it was the glaring absence of an important few that propelled me further into distress.

> Dear Friend who never had the courage to reach out to me after my sister died,
>
> Thank you! You taught me a *very* valuable lesson that will help so many people in our same situation. Upon the return from my sister's house after tending to her family and memorial, you avoided me. It wasn't horrendous. I simply noticed your absence. During moments of clear thinking I wondered where you were or if you

had heard the news. I was baffled that our daily interactions ceased to exist. Were you out of the country? Did something bad happen that I wasn't aware of?

About a month later, we drifted into each other outside of the supermarket. After the typical hug and greetings, you grabbed my hands and said it was not in your nature to know what to say when someone suffers a tragedy, so you said nothing. I told you that I understood, gave you a wide smile and we parted ways. The fact is that I did understand but I didn't like it one bit. Our situation gave me so much to think about, and it was a good thing, too, because when my lovely friend lost her sweet boy 10 months later, I knew how I needed to act.

My lesson for us is: when a friend loses a loved one, merely saying, "I am so sorry," and/or, "Can I do anything for you?" works like a gem. Ignoring them because you don't know what to say only leads to more sadness. The hug with no words was also perfect for me. When people acknowledged my loss, I felt cared about and loved during a time of severe grief. Everyone is different, indeed. If your friends want to be left alone, write a meaningful letter that says, "I am always here for you." Keep up the note sending on a regular basis, letting them know that you are thinking of them. You can always send random gift cards for a coffee of their choice when they are up to being in the world again. It depends upon who that person is, however, at a minimum, it is perfect to simply say that you care.

I care about you.

Love,
Wendy

Chapter Two –

Remorse

The pit in my stomach creates a sensation that fills my entire body with nausea. I feel a deep sense of anxiety mixed with regret, which makes my breath shallow and my heart beat faster. This chapter on remorse is filled with letters that are deeply apologetic. I may never be able to speak these words out loud to the specific parties that need to hear them, however the simple act of figuring out what I've done wrong and writing it down makes the sudden panic of regret dim ever so slightly. First step: awareness and realization. Next step: admission. Final step: forgiving myself.

On Being Mean

Ugh. I hate when I'm mean. I wish I could eliminate this behavior permanently from my life. I especially wish that I were able to take back some childhood nastiness that truly wasn't necessary. I've always been a genuinely kind person, but there were bouts of unpleasantness of which I am deeply ashamed. I'm not sure who originally said this, but at the bank they have a sign that states, "It takes forty-two muscles to frown and only seven to smile." Smile with me, people.

Dear Childhood Friends to whom I was mean,

For the life of me I can't figure out why I did some mean things as a kid. I really wasn't a very obnoxious child. Adults liked me and I was often selected to be the student to show the new kid around. I was told often that my warm smile and kind eyes made people feel welcomed. However, as I dig deep to write these letters and figure out exactly who I am, the moments of remorse appear eagerly to be rectified.

There was this one terrible incident that makes me feel so ashamed. When I imagine the mortified look on your innocent face as you became aware of the prank, I am flooded with guilt. You were this kind-hearted girl who wouldn't hurt a fly. Why on earth I chose to spread dog doo all over your bicycle seat truly can't be justified or even explained. While it wasn't my idea, I am equally to blame because my hands were involved in the prank.

We neighborhood girls thought we were so tricky. The prior night we had a sleepover without you, filled with laughter and limited sleep. It wasn't until the first spotting of daylight that one of us had the idea to spread a pile of stinking poo on your polka-dotted banana bike seat. We all shimmered with glee. Yes! Let's do it! You and your fancy bike. Shiny, purple frame with sparkling white handlebars and those plastic, glitter streamers that swayed as you rode down the street. I used to peer behind the curtains of my mom's bedroom and watch the smile on your face grow bigger with every push of your pedals. I'd usually join you on my used, creaking, bike that was a hand-me down from a family friend. It too was purple with groovy flower stickers on the frame, but it paled in comparison to that brand new, birthday bike sitting at the foot of your driveway.

The day of the infamous "doody spreading" was simply a childhood prank fueled by jealousy. In truth, we were all friends, but that day we insisted on acting like idiots. That day we were unkind and thoughtless children who picked up old, filthy dog doo in an odd-shaped oak leaf, and spread it on your pristine bike seat. I remember the foul-smelling package being smeared across the yellow and purple dots, with the dark brown poo seeping out the edges of the leaf, getting our fingers covered in the same mess. Not well-thought out at all. It was absolutely nasty, ending with us tearing-ass down the street, our hands flailing as we made it to the water spigot just in time to evade a passing car. You never found out that it was us, or maybe your kind-hearted nature just had you pretend in front of your mom so we would be spared the consequences.

I wasn't a bully, but there were many of you kids that I didn't give the time of day. Besides the secret doody event, I never really did anything outwardly rude. However, I was crystal clear that there was a hierarchy of popularity and I stayed with the girls near the top. This required me to ignore you and pretend you didn't exist. Yet, you did.

I hope you can accept my apology. I'm sorry if I ever laughed at you for being different. I'm sorry if I never stood up for you when others were saying mean things. I'm sorry for acting like you were nonexistent. I'm sorry that I didn't take the time to get to know you and become your friend. I'm sorry that after six years in elementary school, I pretended like we were utter strangers as we made our way through middle school. I could have been nicer. I could have smiled and made things different. But I chose to remain with the pack.

None of it, I can ever take back. All I can do is try and help the generations of girls behind me to be kinder, better friends. I've spent many years teaching girls how to be strong personal advocates of what they believe is right, through my work with a program called Youth Leadership. I have sat on the streets sharing melting ice cream with homeless, transient girls, getting to know their dreams and helping them to strategize a way to rebuild their lives and make it back to their families. Most importantly, I teach every girl in my life some simple, basic tenets of successful living: a) as human beings, our role is to make the world a better place. This involves raising people up and not tearing them down; b) we all want to be loved and enjoy having friends, remember this and act on it; c) the most important way you can grow is to figure out what is amazing about you. Everyone has gifts, skills, and talents. Find yours and use them. Be AMAZING!

Finally shedding the lingering bits of remorse,
Wendy

On Accepting Cruelty as a Childhood Norm

Everyone wants to be liked and loved. Every child, everywhere, deserves a friend. There is no one in the world that wakes up in the morning with hopes to be the butt of embarrassing jokes. When I spend time thinking about adolescent cruelty I feel sick to my stomach. Sadness and disgust start to bubble up and most usually I push the thoughts away. However, this is not possible today.

I want to make things right for every teen that feels alone, and I want to scream from a mountain top to tell them to care about each other. I don't want another child to take their own life because someone else doesn't like them.

Studies about human psychology have long refuted the idea that aggressive behavior is something one is born with. At some point in the early development of a child, we figure out how to keep others small so that we may feel better. Yet, deep inside, we really don't feel any happier. We might even actually feel worse. That is, if we have properly attached as an infant and developed an empathetic brain (See: On the Importance of Attachment).

I desire every child to wake up in the morning and feel loved, safe, and wanted. I wish for them to have friends and laughter in their life. I want to see girls being complimentary and supportive of each other, and boys accepting other kids that might not be handsome or athletic. I crave for them to learn mediation skills when a problem is detected, so they can sort through hurt feelings and move forward together. Call me unrealistic if you must, but it's still my dream.

Dear Adults Everywhere,

You might not think this letter applies to you, but it does. As adults, we have incredible power, and with it comes deep responsibility. Our primary role is to teach children how to contribute to the greater good of the world and create successful, happy lives.

How have we allowed childhood cruelty to continue with such severe momentum that has lead to staggering teenage suicide statistics? How is this not our collective problem to be addressed with the same vigilance as standardized testing scores? How has it become something that together we can't change or help to heal?

I'm definitely an idealist. No doubt about that. Yet my fundamental belief that every person deserves to have a friend, feel safe, and loved is not too far off the mark. One might say at this point that in my previous letter I too exhibited unkind, alienating behavior as a kid. That is most certainly true, with the key focus on why it was acceptable. I know adults saw us girls being excluding and pitiless, yet I only heard the phrases, "how would you like it if that was done to you" (not very impactful); "kids will be kids" (lame way to avoid doing anything); "c'mon just be her friend" (teens do the opposite). One might even remember that my own son wasn't always nice to his peers. It's true. And guess what? I needed help in helping him. Much as I tried alone, it wasn't possible.

Social acceptance fuels EVERYTHING in a pre-teen/teen existence. We need to make understanding each other and building a strong foundation of accepting others a high priority. Researchers have long found that people have a fundamental need to belong. In the last five years, research is now pointing to how the need to belong is as strong as the need for the physical body to have food and water.

Join with me in an attempt to represent the cure. It will take more than pockets of us in various cities to create a standard where accepting cruelty as a childhood norm becomes a thing of the past. Let's come together in groups of ten and twenty to teach little kids HOW to be a kind, mindful friend. Let's make it SO IMPORTANT to care about each other. This way, we won't think it is someone else's problem the next time we hear of a horrific report of bullying. We can show children ways to see the gifts and talents of every other child (much like they do in kindergarten) and create the custom of celebrating and including, rather than excluding and isolating the ones who are different.

I know it's not a simple answer but we owe it to the future of humanity to try. I don't want to participate in one more conversation about how the middle school age is so tough on kids. I want it to be different, and it starts right here and now.

Join me,
Wendy

P.S . Check out these web sites as a place to start in your advocacy work:

    www.dosomething.org
    www.randomactsofkindness.org
    www.findingkind.com
    www.servicespace.org

On Truth in Jest

Saying something awful to encourage laughter from bystanders is horrible. The sting of the words rips away pieces of ourselves even if the person was "just joking." When someone points out our flaws or mistakes just to get a giggle, it is purely a vile activity. I have found myself as the butt of the joke left only with a crimson-colored, embarrassed face and the feeling of being a little less loved in the world.

Humiliated, embarrassed, disgraced, shamed, dishonored, and degraded are more likely how a person feels after being made fun of for a joke. Making fun of someone is hardly ever followed by joy, delight, honor, and gratitude. No one I know has ever gushed a heartfelt thank you after being put on the spot by someone else's ridicule.

The tagline, "I was only kidding" is garbage. William Shakespeare once said, "In jest, there is truth," and he was right.

I learned this one the hard way.

Dear High School Friend,

I am definitely paying the price for the "joke" I played on you when we were in high school. It's many, many years later and all I can think of when I hear your name is how embarrassed I am by what I did. On your yearbook picture, I wrote something as a joke, but in fact, it was horribly mean. You see, I grew up in a household where making fun of each other was a regular family past time. We took turns at family functions ridiculing each other, in order to get the crowd into hysterics. I was pretty good at it. Maybe you remember this. I'm sure you even got a laugh with my family at my expense.

It wasn't until I was about 27 years old when I found out that there was absolutely nothing funny or honorable about saying mean things to someone, even if you lightheartedly say, "I was just kidding."

My fiancée scolded me once after a party, asking why I insisted on making fun of him every time we were within earshot of a group. I was pretty stunned, being that I had no clue I was hurting his feelings. It was how I was programmed. I believed that making others laugh at the expense of someone else was fine if you were only kidding around. It didn't phase me if their essence began to shrivel in front of your eyes, bravely hiding their humiliation.

I had no strong retort to his inquiry other than it was how I was raised. At parties, the same scenario would play out again and again. I'd hold court and begin to share silly yet embarrassing stories of him. Everyone would be cracking up, me included. I'd think I was the belle of the grand ball with the guests reveling around in my hilarity.

He'd be furious.

After nearly one full year of these disheartening conversations, I finally realized that there was nothing kind, loving, or even remotely interesting about making someone the butt of the joke. It became a high priority for me to completely stop doing this despicable activity.

It was at this point when I thought of you. I am so sorry that you probably never open up that beautiful remembrance of high school because I wrote HORRIBLE and supposedly humorous words by your picture. At the time, I thought it was hysterical. However, I learned later on that it was in fact repulsive and wrong. This is the one thing that I've done in my life that shames me to the core.

I wish I could take it back.

Love,
Wendy

On Regrets

The entire chapter on remorse captures moments in my life when I have acted poorly, or purposefully caused harm to another. This next letter does not follow that same context, yet its lingering effects in my life have been staggering. Regret can be defined as a missed opportunity of which you feel wretchedness over. It's true, I have the sadness, and yes, the opportunity was blatantly missed. However, it was so intensely complicated and painful that I continue to remain stuck. I am able to do so many things to rectify, though I choose none. I hope one day I can find the path to mend and move forward.

Dear You,

This is short because we've yet to reconcile. Three years have passed with both of us silent and wholly removed from each other's world. There are so many things wrong with this situation; I can barely craft a list. I can only say what I regret.

I am deeply sorry for us being out of a relationship for so long. I am sorry that I was compelled to be honest when you asked me a startling question; I answered it truthfully, which created an enormous rift between us. I realize that it may never get repaired and this lifetime may end without us ever getting the chance to speak again. You are proud and I am very unsure.

I am sorry that you and I had a deep connection over the years, and that we are now -nothing. I am most sorry that you have beautiful children that I have no relationship with. I am sorry that I have chosen a "side", but when "sides" got taken, the only place for me to be was where I stood. That was not the side you were on nor will you ever be. I do not know how to move forward, and yet, in my heart, I am so deeply sorry.

I walked around for months in shock, thinking I am not the kind of person that holds a grudge, so why is this one happening? Still, I've yet to find the words to restore our bruised egos and broken hearts.

 I am sorry that there has not been a time to mend the past and begin anew. I hope and imagine that you are living the life of your dreams with extraordinary success. While the time might not be now, there is always a twinkle in my heart that we will someday find the right words with the perfect amount of humility to be us again.

Love and happiness to you always and forever,
Wendy

Chapter Three –

Love Letters

If you have ever been the recipient of a love letter, then you have hopefully felt the burst of sudden joy that emanates from your heart as the words of endearment are presented. In my opinion, there is no greater gift. I have been fortunate to receive a few love letters in my life. There were the notes captured in between the fluorescent hallways as we high school students rushed to reach our next class. Words filled with the promise of young love kept me feeling secure during the uncomfortable teenage years. There were notes from my husband in the beginning days of our relationship, in which he would mail cartoons, articles, and jokes, always titled, "Hi Sunshine." As soon as I would spot the handwriting, everything would feel brighter and better. My cousin may tell you that while she was muddling through her first semester of being a freshman in college, she received letters of adoration from me, helping her to transition away from the comfort of our family, into a world of strangers.

The best love letter I ever received was from Donna, three months prior to her death. Our mother had been suddenly hospitalized after contracting a food-borne illness that nearly took her life. After days on end of my sitting vigil with mom in the hospital, I received the following text from my big sister. "*Hi Wen*. I was just texting Tim how mom is and I found myself writing what a great job you are doing and how grateful I am that you are with her. Thought I should tell you. I don't say enough how I see the hard work you do for others. But I do see it. Mom is very fortunate. So is Roman."

After a lifetime of seeking approval from my older sister, this note was the most gratifying set of loving words I had ever received. On April 7, 2011, five days after the accident, I remembered to find that text and send a copy to myself so that I would be able to hear these words forever. I use them as a reminder that I am now the only daughter, and with that comes a welcomed responsibility.

> You and I need more love letters. Let's all commit to sending spontaneous, juicy sentiments of love to people who have influenced us or touched our lives.

On Safety

Dear Mom,

Who would have ever believed that something positive could have come out of losing Donna, but as I write this letter, I realize that it is indeed so. Had Donna not been instantaneously ripped from our lives, I might not have ever thought of the idea to write this letter to you. Never again do I want to be in the awful predicament of not having said all of the loving words that I have for the special people in my life.

You have been a great mother. It was not easy for you, I realize now. With a blended family, and four teenagers all running at high speeds, it's hard to imagine how you managed. In my mind's eye, times were not always kind to me. I lived a harsh, private, pained childhood wondering what I did wrong to always feel so alone. Yet, despite the hardships, you raised me to be a thoughtful, kind, and an open-minded high achiever. Far back in my elementary years, you taught me that all people are created equal regardless of their skin color or culture. You showed me how to appreciate the people in our community and how to be kind to them.

Things were tough for us in an era when single mothers were non-existent, but the underlying notion that I was loved and special always shone through. Thank you for teaching me how to be generous and to treat people to the material enjoyments of life. I am good at sharing, and I attribute this to you.

You have been my constant source of comfort for almost five decades. I know that with you in the world, I am safe.

Love,
Wendy

Letter from Donna

I can barely get through this letter from Donna without a struggle to hold back the tears. The gooey, pumpkin-carving moments described by my sister are also favorite times of mine that yielded a sense of comfort. My mother did a brilliant job of providing a heart full of memories that will carry on through her grandchildren. This tiny, silly tradition of carving pumpkins and toasting the salted seeds at the kitchen table is our generational commitment to relationship building. Cleaning out the guts, washing the seeds, salting and placing them in the oven is something that both my sister and I handed down to our children. It's really not about the activity, but about the ritual, which illuminated closeness, safety, and a sense of knowing who has your back.

[Thursday, October 29, 1998 11:25am]

Hi Mom & Wen,

The other day I was a chaperone to a pumpkin farm with Taylor's class. When we got to the big pumpkins, Taylor told everyone about how when his mommy was a little girl she would sit at the kitchen table with his grandma and Aunt Wendy and pick the seeds out of the pumpkin goop. What a lovely story to be handed down.

This morning I carved my first adult pumpkin

with my children. Although we didn't have plastic aprons, an oilcloth tablecloth, or a great window view, we did have fun. I was also the only one digging out the seeds because both my sons took one look at it, proclaimed "yuck", and promptly left for the TV. However, I was left with my pumpkin goop and memories of a great time long ago.

Now the seeds are in the oven and I wanted to tell you both that I was thinking of you. I miss those days.

Love,
Donna.

On Unconditional Love

In 2005, my husband, the kids, and I stumbled into the house after a day at the beach to find Ted, our hundred-pound Collie-Shepherd, jimmied in between the speaker stand and the TV in the corner of the living room. A vase was shattered on the floor by his oversized back paws. His labored breathing and weakened heartbeat got us moving very quickly. Within minutes, our boys were safely tucked at the neighbors, and we were en route to the vet. As Ted took his last few breaths on the cold, marble floor of the examination room, the silence in my head was deafening. Tears streamed in continued droplets down my cheeks while we both privately thanked him for a decade of joy.

The loss of Ted taught me so much. As an adult, I had never experienced a beloved pet dying, and it felt wretched. I sat for days reminiscing and recognizing the unconditional love which exists between animal and human. Ted's death gave me an opportunity to consciously distinguish the impact that unconditional love from a pet has on human beings.

In 2010, a beagle puppy was picked up as he was running down I-95 in South Florida. He was brought to a local, no-kill animal shelter near the location in which he was recovered. By the time I stumbled upon him, he had been there for months. It was a quiet Saturday with both boys at friend's houses. I had the luxury of being in the car alone with my thoughts and music. That day, I had just been wandering about and got a sudden urge to visit the shelter. Nothing much came of the trip, other than me snapping a photo of this adorable dog behind the metal fencing. About 30 days later, we formally decided to adopt a second dog, and my husband called from the shelter requesting my presence to check out his pick. It was serendipitous that the dog he selected was the same little beagle staring at me through the fence a month prior. Five years later, I still feel a twinge of sadness for the people that lost this marvelous animal. Sometimes, silently I speak to them as I pet his sleepy head and listen to his soft snores.

Dear Previous Owners of the lost dog we adopted,

I love your dog! He is my absolute best friend. I know that he did not run away from you, because the day we adopted him, he jumped into my lap in the driver's seat of the car and only wanted to sit there. I imagine that you taught him this behavior, because most dogs don't naturally gravitate towards the lap of the driver with their nose contentedly facing the wind. You must have been devastated when Buddie ran away. It's that curious beagle nose! He's done it to us many times, too, but always manages to come back. The first time he took off, he had caught scent of some critter at the edge of the mangrove trees where we were taking a walk. In a split second he was gone, and all we could hear was the faint clinging of his dog tags as he chased his new toy in splendor. We ran/walked for hours through the spider webs and possible snakes in the swampy Florida trails, with my son and I stopping to pray, cry, and plead. Within minutes of us returning to the car for a refill of water, I heard the jingle of his collar coming towards us. The relief was immense.

As I write this letter, I stop to bury my head in the folds of his neck-fur as he is sleeping. He exhales a deep sigh. I love this dog. I'm sorry for your loss, but I'm thrilled for my gain. Buddie is the most joyous, dedicated, sensitive, happy, loving dog I have ever met. He is my best friend. I will always keep him safe and treasured.

Love,
Wendy

On Feeling Loved

My hope is for everyone to experience deep love from another person. To be clear, I do not mean the Cinderella type of love with a prince riding on a white horse, but the kind that demonstrates you are not alone in this world. A love where someone else helps you to be the best you can be. A love that allows you to feel valued, respected, adored, and appreciated. Feeling loved by my husband is not the kind you see on the movie screen with Hugh Grant and Julia Roberts. It is the kind of love that worries when I'll be home, shares quiet confidences, and emanates a deep sense of respect for our commitment to each other.

Dear Marc,

People might think that writing a love letter to your husband of almost twenty years might be the easiest to compose, but as I begin the task, it seems the most daunting. We see each other in the greatest of moments and the ugliest of times. Some people may think I am joking when I share that on the day I first laid eyes on you, time stopped. And while you don't admit it, I saw you experience that same moment. You were wearing a navy blue, crew neck shirt – standing in the center of the reception room, quickly turning around to see who came in the door. As the bride and I entered the room, our eyes met. Time stopped. Everything came to an abrupt halt. As fast as it came, the moment passed, and was not recalled until days later when we met again at the wedding.

Being married and committed to each other has been the absolute greatest part of my life. Your bellowing laughter is contagious, causing us more times than not to make spectacles of ourselves in the most inappropriate times. Your deep, soulful brown eyes that look incredibly similar to our beloved first dog, Barkley, instantly make my heart sing. The fact that we both believe this to be a compliment allows me to smile widely.

You have been the most selfless, supportive husband and friend, silently and sometimes not-so-silently, helping me to figure out my purpose and then quietly watching as I make it come to fruition. If it weren't for you, I would have never had the courage to start a consulting business and continue it for almost 20 years.

Now that I take the time to do this, I realize that many of my life's greatest accomplishments were because YOU had the notion for us to do something. Most importantly, you directed us towards the adoption of our own darling children. It was that generous heart of yours that led us to them. Thank God for you.

Last year, on the anniversary of Donna's death, you gave me a two-inch book of every email that she and I wrote to each other, stemming back to 1994. How you managed to rifle through all of those emails and accounts I will never know, but to receive that perfectly bound testament of caring illustrates exactly why you are the only man for me.

Love,
Honey

Letter from Donna

Love is about seeing someone else happy. It involves a selfless generosity that comes naturally. Love lets us support each other and celebrate the fabulous attributes that only you deliver in this world. My sister loved me.

[Sunday, July 6, 1997 10:27am]

Hi Wendy.

It's funny, even though we live far from each other I miss you when you are out of town. I've been anxiously awaiting your return so that we can email again. I want to hear all about your honeymoon. I'm so glad you guys had a great time. I had a blast at the wedding. Both of us did. I can't wait to see the video.

You were so beautiful and I've never seen such a tremendous smile on Marc's face as I did when you came down the aisle. I'm excited that we may see you next week. We'll have a meatless barbeque for you.

Love, Donna

On Comfort

The pure act of giving and receiving comfort takes only one thing – LOVE. After Donna's tragic passing, I had a vision in mind of how to be comforting to my sister's teenage sons. I wanted to hold them on my lap as I did when they were babies and never let them go. I wanted them to know and feel through me that their mother is still with them and will always be. Yet, they were teenagers with full lives and lived many hours away from my home. I had to alter my original vision and do whatever I could when each moment presented itself.

It is here that I think of my dear brother-in-law who has done a miraculous job of picking up the shards from their mom's death, while in the midst of losing his wife. He alone has insisted and created their lives to become normal and meaningful again. Every day, I send my sister's boys comfort, love, and the intention that they blossom into the vision that my sister held for them.

Dear Taylor,

I can't tell you how sorry I am for the loss of your mom. The world without your mom seems lifeless and dull. I can only imagine how it is for you. When you were born, you gave your mother the greatest gift of all time. Not only did she feel the joy that all new, first-time mothers have, but she finally experienced a complete sense of peace that she had been searching for her whole, entire life. It seemed to everyone that knew her that she was finally free.

What joy, to be considered the gift in someone else's life. That was you... your mom's private gift to herself and the world! Your mom loved you so incredibly much. It was through her relationship with you that she uncovered her own personal truth, and how to help other moms be as amazing as she.

I told your dad about the book of letters between your mom and myself, and we decided that someday when the time was right, I would share it with you and your brother. Until then, here are some of her words to tide you over:

[Tuesday, September 3, 1996 at 4:34pm]

Hi Wen. Taylor had his first big loss today. Who would have guessed it would be a shoe? It was an absolutely glorious day with a light breeze and no clouds. The kids were having a blast playing in the sand and we were tossing them about in the waves (holding on, of course, this is the Atlantic). Then it happened... Taylor's pool shoe came off.

I saw it go into the wave and made a lunge for it, but it was swept up in the undertow. He cried and cried bitterly that he wanted his pool shoe. It was so sad. The poor child was inconsolable. He finally fell asleep on the way home, but as he was shutting his eyes, his looked up at me mournfully and said that he wanted his pool shoe back.

Two and a half hours later, I see him lying on the bed looking very sad. He was still mourning his pool shoe, so I made up a story about how when I was little the ocean gobbled up my favorite red sand shovel and he started to laugh.

Then we went to Caldor's for another pair (which I knew they wouldn't have at this time of year) but we did find a pair of Winnie the Pooh sandals that made him very happy. $1.80 later, and he was happy again, although I was really sad because at one point I blew it with him. I was trying to be empathetic and supportive. I do believe that when a child is feeling something you should let him feel it. Well, we were trying to leave and get everything together and Taylor was just a mess. I kept saying over and over that I was sorry and that I knew that he was sad but I couldn't get him his shoe back and kept offering to buy a new pair.

Finally my frustration was mounting because he was just standing there sobbing looking at the ocean. There was no way that I could carry him and he was not cooperating and I finally scolded him and said, "Ok. Taylor, it's enough already," with major emphasis on *enough*. He quieted down after that but I felt awful. I broke one of my diehard rules.

Thankfully, he started up again when we got to the parking lot so I just dropped all of my things, picked him up and rocked him until he was finished. I still feel badly. Big lesson learned. Have to find patience no matter what especially when kids are hurting. They have to go through it (with you) or they will internalize it. So that's my story. – Donna

Please, please, please call me whenever you need to; it doesn't matter the time, day, year, or century. I will come running.

Love, LOVE, Love,
Aunt Wendy

Dear Will,

Perfect as you are, my love, you came into this world with a big show. Your mom tells the story like this: her back was hurting, and she went to the downstairs bedroom to make herself more comfortable. Next thing she knew she was in active labor with no time to spare. Within a very short time frame you were born in the house with the assistance of a New Jersey Police Officer!

I remember her being mortified that she was giving birth with someone that might pull her over for running a red light one day – but that was quickly overtaken by her immense joy of having YOU. Oh, you were such a beautifully plump baby. We all couldn't wait to hold and carry you – including your brother! William, your mom loved you so much. She spent every waking day and night searching for ways to make your life balanced and happy. She believed down to the core that her job was to figure out what you needed and to get it for you. She would have climbed Mt. Everest, barefoot, if that meant you would be safe and care-free.

Below is an email one week after you came into this world.

[Sunday, December 29, 1996 at 1:01pm]

Hi Wen. Mom is coming tomorrow. We will go to the pediatrician in the am. It will be my first excursion alone with the boys. Oh gosh... the boys! My sons, the kids, how cool! Tim took the greatest picture yesterday which I am hoping he got in focus. Taylor was sitting on my lap and I had to nurse William. He wouldn't get up so I shifted him so I could do both. Well, Taylor curled his body around William and rested his head on top of the baby's. It was one of those perfect moments in life. William is the best. I am so in love with this little peanut. He is a really good baby. He is tolerant and pretty quiet and even his cries are adorable. He's not a loud crier. Actually his preamble to anger is squeaking. I can't wait for you to see him. He is really cute and cuddly. Well that's about all. Love ya, Taylor and William's mom.

I want you to know from that day until forever: I will always be someone you can count on. It does not matter if we don't talk often, or if we haven't seen each other in months. You are my sister's baby and that makes you my baby too.

Love you until the end of time,
Aunt Wen

Chapter Four –

Letters of Judgment

You know what makes me crazy? When people say, "I'm not judging, I'm just saying." Really? You aren't judging when you have an opinion about something? Uh, yeah you are. Judging is a way to dissect information to understand what you think about a topic. I judge to determine if the road I'm on is the one I want to drive on or not. Judging is a significant part of life and keeps us safe. Pretending that you don't have strong opinions that sway you is ludicrous.

Oops, not judging you – just saying.

This chapter is about my judgments. They are purely my opinions. Does that make them right? Who the hell cares? As long as I'm not hurting anyone else or being unkind, then I figure it is okay.

The letters in this chapter are a collection of my opinions based on what is true for me. If they resonate with you, great – we can be judgmental together. If not, dig deep – unleash your issues and join me on the other side, in freedom.

On the Importance of Attachment

There is no manual on parenting, and I could have seriously used one. I found myself in the middle of the transition from professional to parent, sitting cross-legged on the fluffy brown carpeting in the den, miserable and lonely. My boys were home from Russia for about two months, and during nap time all I could do was wonder if other exhausted mothers felt the same way I did?

Parenting is so difficult. There is no instruction manual and we are expected to innately know the way. I found myself in this judging/deciphering mode. Am I alone? Does everyone have an overwhelmed little guy who can't touch certain things? Did anyone else's child have such a difficult time being in close quarters with other children that within ten minutes they had sunk their teeth deeply into the arm, shoulder, or leg of another? Does anyone feel like crying all day long?

True, adopting two boys, ages 20 months and three, was a completely different scenario. Yet, there had to be some similarities between myself and other moms. Of course, I was too ashamed to ask for help because most moms around me looked like they had it together. So I did it alone. After years of quietly working at mothering, I became resentful. I got angry at parents who for one reason or another did things that were neglectful of their child's growth, and then pretended that because the baby was little, it was fine. As the person who still deals with cleaning up the mess that someone else caused one of my babies, I can tell you that every moment in a child's little life matters.

Dear New and Prospective Parents,

If you don't think that what you do during the first year of your baby's life matters, you are nuts. What you put in your body while pregnant and how connected you are to your baby's needs, definitely matters.

I have single-handedly repaired the mess that was made of my son before he came to me at 20 months, simply due to a lack of caring when he was a baby. I can PROMISE you that during the attachment cycle, your baby is developing an ability to trust and build empathy for others during those years. When you repeatedly ignore a baby, and the baby's brain experiences their needs not being met, a serious cycle of mistrust gets initiated. Believing that an infant can't process neglect or that they will never remember something, is way off base. People need to read about the attachment cycle and how it pertains to helping the next generation become an empathetic, contributing set of individuals, before they even consider having sex. Then maybe we won't have so many consciously and unconsciously neglected kids running around wreaking havoc in their own lives.

And, while we are on the subject: DON'T EVEN CONSIDER smoking a cigarette around your child's forming lungs. What a freaking dumb idea.

I know I'm being judgmental, yet it's said with a lot of love for your kids,

Wendy

Letter from Donna

Donna spent her entire experience during motherhood always searching for ways to help her children thrive. There were so many things that she and I did not see eye-to-eye on, but parenting was not one of those things. She was the smartest mother, and taught me incredibly useful things that helped me raise two honorable, young men.

[Friday, September 28, 2007 9:37pm]

Hi Wen,

Just remember, allow the personalities and abilities of your children to guide your expectations. Wanting your child to get A's when they don't have the ability will only frustrate them and end up causing attitude and rebellion. Celebrate the little triumphs like bringing homework home and reading/understanding the story.

Above all RELAX! You cannot control their learning abilities but you sure can foster and encourage them to do their best. Reward their achievements. Perhaps you can create a simple chart. A star for every time they do something school related. Five stars earns a treat. Set up expectations that they can achieve. Make them easy at first and once they get the hang of it you can increase the tasks. Encourage, encourage, encourage.

Someone once told me not to treat my kids like little adults. They are little kids. Keep it simple and love on them a lot. It was good advice. I still have to remember it.

Call me anytime. This is one of the hardest things you will have to do. Let go of what you want and help them be what they can be. Then watch them blossom.

Love,
Donna

On the Right Thing Happening

For an entire summer, I gave myself permission to contemplate what it would feel like if my husband and I never became parents. I read the book, *Sweet Grapes: How to Stop Being Infertile and Start Living Again* by Jean & Michael Carter, and for those two months, eliminated the stress of fertility testing. It was a mind-blowing process until my sister showed up for a weeklong visit in August with both of her boys in tow. Her love for her children was contagious and seeped into me. Directly after they departed, our quest to raise our own children continued. It was not easy but it was purposeful and the faces of my beautiful boys remind me to earnestly believe in the power of faith.

Dear Some People in my world,

Years ago when Marc and I started the adoption process, it all seemed so incredibly daunting. Our private and very unpleasant battle with fertility procedures had finally come to an end with the hope of adoption. The process of adoption is so filled with raw emotion and an overload of paperwork. Each step had to be done with self-reflection, precision, accuracy, and a notary, yet that wasn't even truly the overwhelming part. The difficulty lay in my interactions with some of you. Nearly every other person that I came in contact with revealed their own personal fear and uncertainty through careless questions continually fired at me.

It wasn't the actual questioning that was so awful; it was the permeation of your uncertainty that started to bleed onto me. About two months into the process, with a collection of papers that could light a house on fire, I found myself staring at the wall in my office and I could barely breathe. What was I so anxious about? It truly wasn't the adoption proceedings because I felt clear and confident. Well, then... what in the heck was it?

I immediately phoned Donna to unload my burden. I still wasn't crystal clear about where my anxiety was coming when she simply told me, "you need to find your faith." After an additional 30 minutes, I realized the problem. Your fears were seeping into my certainty and I was letting them make me afraid. Questions like, "how do you know?" and, "aren't you afraid?" or comments such as, "my husband would never adopt children," were piling up in my psyche and cluttering my heart. It was in that immediate moment of revelation when my sister's words made sense, and I found the phrase, "the right thing will happen." All of a sudden things started to make sense, and it was like a bright light was blinking wildly over my head. I felt excited and at the same time oddly serene. I was willing to try anything to get rid of the anxiety that wasn't even mine to begin with.

Slowly over time, when the questions would occur

– and they most certainly did, I simply answered, "the right thing will happen". I said it to anyone and everyone. Anytime you asked, "what will you..." or "are you sure that..." I answered, "the right thing will happen".

One of the most amazing aspects of the human brain is that when you give it an idea, it will believe that idea if you repeat it enough. It's called learning. So without emotion or disbelief, I fully embraced the concept that the right thing will happen. I taught myself to BELIEVE and to remove doubt from the learning process. My life became my own again, and we were able to completely enjoy the journey.

I realize that many of you don't know me personally; however you must trust me when I tell you that THE RIGHT THING HAPPENED. I found the two babies that we spent 15 months searching for. There is zero doubt in my mind that they were meant for us and we were meant for them. Ask anyone who knows us and they will tell you so. Even my dear friend's 11 year old daughter told me two weeks after their arrival home that it felt like they had been with us forever.

If you are a non-believer that the right thing will happen for you, then take it from me. When you put your mind to it and push away every ounce of disbelief, you can make things come true that are right for you. Keep moving forward step by step, eliminating fear and it's bound to happen.

Congratulations for entering the next phase of awesomeness. I am here to tell you that you can have what you want in this life. My boys are your proof.

With much love from an eternally *grateful* mom, Wendy

On Helping Others

Have you ever been the recipient of unwarranted assistance? Has someone ever done something for you without being asked? It's such a marvelous experience. I wish we did it more.

Dear Potential Helpers of the world,

Remember the moment during childhood when some random adult called us a good little helper and it felt incredible? It was nearly the highest compliment that a kid could receive. For some reason, as we grew older, we began to value helping others less. I met a woman several years ago in a high-powered, fascinating job, who whispered in my ear at a meeting, how does a person begin to volunteer? I found it curious that the concept of helping, which was a significant foundation of our younger lives, became so foreign to many of us.

There are a huge number of ways to help other people. You can simply call the nonprofit organization of your choice (see the On Dedication section for some neat ideas of amazing projects) and tell them that you would like to help. You may need to wait a few weeks for a return call, so be patient. There are also thousands of informal ways to be a helper in the world. You could assist an elderly neighbor, hold the door for someone, give your seat on the bus to another person, pay for a stranger's drink, babysit for a friend who needs some recuperation time, pick up trash in your neighborhood, or simply smile at anyone you see.

A neighbor of mine, years back in Colorado, used to shovel the snow up and down the sidewalks of the entire cul-de-sac. I was younger, then, and he made such an impression on me. I found his little bits of neighborhood assistance exceedingly generous, especially for the elderly folks on the street. He was no spring chicken, either. It was a freezing January afternoon with about five inches of snow on the ground when I saw him pass my house, shovel in hand, and with icicles forming on his silver-white beard. It was the day I decided to be just like him.

Join me in emulating my adored neighbor. Find anything you can do in the world to help others, and I will too.

Cheers to our hearts doing great stuff together,

Wendy

On Receiving Compliments

My youngest son whispers to me as we walk through the mall that I am not allowed to share life lessons with strangers. I always agree, but I never pinky promise. I simply can't. Of course I receive a litany of grievances after I've done the deed, but he will tell you later on that he really does think my words have helped the person feel better. Poor kid – with a community organizing mom who loves to make people smile. Not a good recipe for strolling through the mall on a cold, winter afternoon.

Dear Strangers,

When the following conversation begins between the two of us, I can tell by your grimacing face that you think I'm out of my mind. What I love is that by the end of the interaction, we have both learned something valuable. You walk away with a new skill to help you feel fantastic, and I continue my quest for connecting with humanity. Or maybe you walk away with a new person on your lunatic list and I'm still me. Either way works.

Scene: In line for checking out at a store in the mall. My son rolling his eyes behind me, and his deep voice is growling my name. I approach the clerk with my merchandise.

Me: Your eyes are beautiful. [My big smile]

You: Thanks, so are yours. [Your half smile]

Me: I want to share a secret with you. [Son now grabbing my elbow.] When someone gives you a compliment it's always good to just say thank you. When you immediately return a compliment, it doesn't allow you to really feel that someone else just said something fabulous about you. [Your AWKWARD GRIMACE telling me I might be the craziest person you have ever met, but I keep going.] Let's try it again. Your eyes are spectacular. [My largest smile ever]

You: Thank you. [Your authentic smile]

Me: [Walking away feeling slightly foolish, but hopeful that from now on you will allow someone's kind words to penetrate and help uplift your spirit. Younger son's complaints acknowledged and dismissed.]

Thank you,
Wendy

On Showing Off

As a child, there was this thing about me that I couldn't help. I glowed. People gravitated towards me. I enjoyed fun, being carefree, and effervescent. I loved being the center of attention. I was loud. Certain circumstances led to some people repeatedly demanding that I change. I was called a show-off. There were negative opinions shooting at me to stop shining so much. I got the message that it was wrong for me to simply be myself.

This next letter is to encourage us to stop squashing the overly large personalities of children, just because it makes someone uncomfortable. The idea is to help them channel it and use their gifts for good. It took years to pound down my bubbly self into something dark and unrecognizable, but I succeeded. Then it took me years of therapeutic assistance to allow my inner self to percolate back outward.

As a community advocate, organizer, teacher, author, facilitator, and inspirer, these gifts help me to change lives. Let's always bring out the best in each other, especially the children.

Dear "They Say,"

Sometimes circumstances in life will require an immediate life lesson. In many situations, when people don't have a factual basis for something, they might refer to the term "they say" as strong proof for a position. I wonder who "they" are and why "they" are the local authority on everything? One of the lessons that "they said" to me when I was in elementary school was don't brag and don't be a show off. So I didn't. I tried as hard as I could to hide all of my inner talents so as not to shine too brightly, or be too good. It took a couple of years to really perfect my invisibility, which eventually turned into a huge quantity of self-hatred. To be exact: two decades of self-destruction – all to avoid being seen for the greatness that resided inside of me. Sound familiar?

Several years ago while I was working on the Kids at Hope initiative in St. Lucie County, Florida, I came across a school project created by an eight-year-old girl. It was a welcome-back-to-school assignment in which the children were answering the following statement: I am a Kid at Hope because –. Their job was to describe themselves in relation to being skilled, talented, and capable of success (please do check out Kids at Hope, it will change your child's life). This little girl's project made a huge impression on me as the words she chose were: I am funny and brave; I am strong and respectful; I am amazing, I am beautiful, and clever.

When was the last time you referred to yourself as beautiful and clever? I can tell you that from age eight to twenty-five, I used the opposite describe myself. What a shame that I bought the bill of goods that was sold to me by "they." It cost me so much self-love, excitement, joy, friendship, and inner belief, along with completely halting me from becoming my vision of myself.

I, by no means, want to put any coaches or therapists out of business; however, if we discontinue telling the children of the world to stop showing off, there would be less self- esteem problems in the world. Obviously, it's not the cure for everything, but having children celebrate their greatness is something that we should support. It is up to us adults to make sure that each and every child remembers how special and amazing they are. "They say", don't be a show off and I say DO. It's your job in the world to be the best you can be and shine brightly.

Says me,
Wendy

Chapter Five –
Heroes

Who are the people in this enormous world that you strive to emulate? Are there individuals whose presence makes you smile? This chapter includes letters that celebrate the greatness of others. There are countless people doing life-changing work out there. Are you one of them?

On Amazing Adults

Teachers are the most powerful people. They have the ability to captivate and mold the neurological development of a child. They can inspire creativity, compassion, and character, coupled with a desire to know more and strive for greatness. This dynamic is incredible and should be highly valued by the adults who fill these roles. During my older son's early years of education, I encountered a teacher who used every minute of her position to inspire the children. To say it was stunningly remarkable is an understatement. Thank goodness, six years later when my youngest son was in desperate need of an empathetic, understanding instructor, she had miraculously moved to his middle school. This letter is to you: the most impressive, outstanding teacher I have ever met.

Dear Second Grade Teacher of my oldest son,

I remember the precise moment I realized you were the most wonderful teacher I had ever come across. I was volunteering in my oldest son's second grade classroom and you were having the kids demonstrate their "rollercoaster cheer", regarding the success of a classmate reaching an academic achievement. It involved everyone up on their feet, snapping their fingers in wild, circular movements ending in a snap, pop, and kapow! All kids smiling, everyone energized, and feeling fabulously supportive.

This was only one of the dozen or so ways that you encouraged your students to publicly praise the good work of another student. At that specific moment in time, I felt my life change. The pure joy on the faces of the students as well as my own son told me that these kids are going to blossom while they are under your tutelage. I felt grateful that at the early age of eight years old, the kids were learning concepts like feeling inspired, gratitude, acknowledging the accomplishments of others, balancing silly with purposeful action, and simply knowing that an adult believes in their personal success.

To say that our family believes you saved my youngest son's life during 6th grade might actually be an understatement. His ability to make it through the middle school day was completely due to the fact that he had you for two periods in a row. You gave him the space to learn at his pace and because of your respectful nature, always provided the opportunity for him to meet your expectations. You are a gem, a miracle worker, and a teaching phenomenon.

On behalf of every student who has been fortunate enough to be in your class, thank you. You change lives.

Love,
Mrs. Wolff

On Friendship

We were sitting in the auditorium awaiting rehearsal for the elementary age, countywide theatre group. She sat two seats away and was from a school on the other side of town. We briefly knew each other from belonging to the same Temple; however it was here on this day that something inside of me recognized the importance we would have on each other's lives.

Dear Friend since the fourth grade,

This letter is necessary yet none of this will be new for you to hear. We have been best friends for over 35 years with an insane level of honesty that some people would call foolish. Our words with each other are flawless and purposeful. Our laughter is long, private, and bubbles over at the most inappropriate times. Our similarities are precise and our differences are honored. There is no one in the universe like you. You are the smartest, funniest, bravest, kindest, sharpest, gentlest, thoughtful, most underappreciated person I have ever met.

I am SO proud of your accomplishments and am thrilled that I have been able to personally grow because of them. You have helped me understand how to be an advocate for my son in the face of shame and sometimes denial. You have overcome gigantic obstacles with grace, completely on your own. Not many people can say that and really mean it. I am thankful to have watched your process and to have helped to cheer you on when it was looking pretty grim.

I want the world to recognize whom I see, know, and love. I am the luckiest girl on the planet to have a friend like you. You mean the world to me and I can't wait to be old ladies together.

I love you,
Wendy

On Changing the World

My sweet and loving college roommate calls me her personal Oprah Winfrey. My cheeks always redden with embarrassment of even remotely being compared to this mega-role model. I think my friend means that I'm simply the type of person who speaks the truth and is wildly committed to respect, justice, and spreading goodness. What Oprah has done for humanity is exceptionally remarkable. While my friend is sweet, I can only aspire to be able to raise people up in their own lives as Oprah has done for millions of us.

Dear Oprah Winfrey,

What a miracle you are! Some might think that writing a letter to you is simply a marketing ploy to grab your attention, and while that might be an excellent outcome, it is not the reason behind these words.

I wanted to thank you for everything you have done for our world. You brought thought-provoking, spiritually based dialogues to the lives of everyday people, encouraging them to understand and embrace the meaning of faith. How extraordinary that you used the access of your media platform to help millions contemplate their roles as spiritual beings, and develop the ability to nurture one's true self. I love this so much.

We all have our favorite Oprah moments. My first favorite was the show with Glenn Close and Puppies Behind Bars, which connect military personnel who have Post Traumatic Stress Disorder with well-loved service dogs that were expertly trained by prison inmates. I cried throughout the entire show. For years, I cited the double benefits of this program when I trained hundreds of adults to understand that all children are capable of success, regardless of any factors bestowed upon them.

My other absolute favorite Oprah moment was the interview with John Diaz regarding his experience when his flight on Singapore Airlines exploded. I waited for years to see this interview, again to hear how he described seeing the auras of his fellow passengers as they left their bodies. It gave me hope, comfort, encouragement, and reduced my personal fear. A while back, I took my youngest son to get his aura photographed. The absolute craziest thing came through in the photos: both of my deceased dogs were visible in the outer lining of his picture, beyond the bright orange and pink hues surrounding his head. If another friend of mine didn't confirm what I saw, and I never heard John Diaz's interview, I may have missed it.

On behalf of everyone, everywhere thank you.

With admiration,
Wendy Wolff

On Being There

On September 11, 2001, my older brother could not idly sit at home and view the media reports regarding the horrific attack on the United States and our citizens. He somehow managed to make it down to the World Trade Center, pick up a spare fire hat, and work for the next three days clearing rubble and saving people's lives. While everyone was thinking of our losses and lives, he was serving others with humility and benevolence. He is a hero.

Dear Big Brother,

Sometimes, when I think about the childhood moments that warm my heart the most, you inevitably are in the foreground. In my head, I hear Donna saying something about you being a whirlwind of loudness, and while this holds some truth, I find you to be comforting in a time of unmanageable chaos.

You, older brother, are one of the most committed, courageous, dedicated human beings I have ever met. Something extraordinary and honorable inside of you created a way for you to finagle a strategy down to the World Trade Center on September 11th, spending days on end pretending to be a firefighter so you could lend your heart to those in need. YOU did that for strangers, for your country, for me, for us. Amazing!!

Sure, you are garrulous and sarcastic beyond belief. I am the first one to run screaming from a room with my hands over my ears. However you are also the guy that lends money, chauffeurs, asks questions, and is forever available to help.

It isn't a coincidence that you found yourself at 42 years old starting to volunteer for the New York Guard with kids that were the same age as your daughter. It is because deep down, the most important thing to you is a dedication to humanity. You taught me that commitment to people is critical. I saw that in the weekly mandatory Daddy/Daughter dinners that you insisted upon, and I see that now in your dedication to my boys and being in their lives.

I love you. I love your daughter. It is amazing to watch her at a mere 21 years old become this international humanitarian, and yet there is no surprise about it. She learned how to be dedicated to people through you.

Give yourself a huge pat on the back.

Love,
Wendy

On Dedication

For over twenty years, I have worked helping nonprofit organizations improve their operations so that they can provide outstanding programs to people who are in need. My passion for community and organizing began during graduate school at NYU, where I became acquainted with the book, *And the Band Played On*, by Randy Shilts. The community mobilization that occurred in San Francisco around HIV/AIDS was remarkable. It was in that same forum that I read, *Rules for Radicals*, by Saul Alinsky, and realized that I was fervent about the concept of community change and creating opportunities for anyone, anywhere.

I have spent years creating collaborative links between communities in need, and the institutions that provide services. It began in 1993 when I was charged with developing a cohesive HIV coalition in a very conservative Colorado community. My charge was to bring people together whom the disease affected, and create partnerships to respond to the rising incidents of HIV in the community. It was quite a task; however it was there that I learned the meaning of finding commonalities and creating masterpieces from it.

Most recently, I was responsible for implementing a county-wide initiative to change the perspectives of adults from *"children can be successful if they do this, and this,"* to "all children are capable of success no exceptions." The Kids at Hope initiative was brought to Florida by a collaborative of business, government, and nonprofit leaders concerned about the impact of gangs on the county. It was a thorough community change process that began with a handful of people, and by the time I left the project, the county was dedicated to this new belief system and structure. I love the non-profit world. It draws a workforce of dedicated individuals who are incredibly creative and giving, working with very little to create a powerful impact.

Dear People who work with non-profits,

You are the exceptional people of the world! I wanted to simply share how fantastic it is that you have found a way to do great work in the world. Every day, you have dedicated your life to making the world better for those whom you serve. I am in awe of you.

There are millions of people like you throughout the globe who have made the commitment to formally help others, whether it is through providing clean water, reducing violence in neighborhoods, increasing self sufficiency, reducing poverty, increasing access to medical care, building forever families, increasing skills among youth, helping people to heal, or any other cause that changes lives.

I am grateful to you and always honored to volunteer when I can. Thanks for being daily role models for the rest of us.

Kindest regards,
Wendy

A small collection of my favorite organizations is listed below:

350.org
A global movement to helping solve the climate crisis.

National Council for Adoption
Adoption advocacy and awareness services for adoption professionals, families, birth parents, and agencies.

Artists Striving to End Poverty
Connects performing and visual artists with underserved youth in the U.S. and around the world to awaken their imaginations, foster critical thinking, and help them break the cycle of poverty.

Avenue D Boys and Girls Choirs
Offers St. Lucie County youth opportunities to succeed through music.

Dancing Dreams
Gives children with physical challenges a chance to dance.

Dewmore Baltimore
Dedicated to increasing civic engagement among youth and adults to create sustainable change.

Denver Dumb Friends League
An animal rescue organization that provides a strong and steadfast voice for those who cannot speak for themselves.

Doctors without Borders
Doctors and nurses volunteer to provide urgent medical care in countries to victims of war and disaster regardless of race, religion, or politics.

Homeboy Industries
Serves high-risk, formerly gang-involved men and women with a continuum of free services and programs, and operates social enterprises that serve as job-training sites.

The Inner Truth Project
Exists because there is no shame in living through any type of sexual abuse, violence, or rape.

It Takes A Village
Reduces health and social disparities among people of color.

Learning Life Company
Introduces young adults to the real world through involvement with service learning.

Puppies Behind Bars
Trains prison inmates to raise service dogs for wounded war veterans and explosive detection canines for law enforcement.

The Mr. Holland Opus Foundation
Donates musical instruments to under-funded music programs throughout the United States.

Wounded Warrior Project
Provides programs and services to severely injured service members during the time between active duty and transition to civilian life.

On Chance

Call it what you will: chance, fate, coincidence, or perfect timing. I love winding up in the right place at the right time. When I stumbled across the person in this next letter, I was beginning to understand that there is so much I don't know about the future. One day, I decided to adopt the concept that I really don't know what the future has in store for me, so the only route to take is one in which I trust and accept all possibilities. This book being in your hands right now is a concrete result of that philosophy.

Chance and possibility had me find a sparkly, effervescent, and charming woman who is now a colleague and treasured friend. Together, we changed hundreds of lives while working on a community advocacy initiative. Developing a commitment to believing in possibilities led me to this chance encounter, which changed my entire life.

> Dear Sweet Mindi,
>
> About seven years ago I recalled seeing a woman out of the corner of my eye during a shopping spree in Target. Her radiance filled the entire space, and in a fleeting second I felt like I needed to know her. Several hours later, and without remembering the moment, I found my son chattering with her baby at the diner we had

stopped in for lunch.

It was your bright smile and kind eyes that I immediately connected to. I wanted to know you and we quickly formed a fast friendship. Our relationship then turned into work associates, better friends, and ultimately moved into us seeming like sisters.

I love how many people in this world admire you. Without you, a litany of things would not have happened to make my life and the world a better place.

Lesson for the rest of us: never dismiss something before it happens, because chance, coincidence, or perfect timing can change your life.

Love,
Wendy

Chapter Six –

Is this the Best We Can Do?

I am not perfect. I make mistakes. I have been known to use a few bad words during my days. With that said, this next chapter comes from my commitment to make the world a better place.

Making mistakes, poor judgment, bad behavior, outbursts, and impulsive responses are a part of life. The trick is to recognize them as they occur, and set a course of action to change. Sometimes it is easy, sometimes not. Everything we do sets a path for our future. Do yourself a favor, and start reading the work of authors like Wayne Dyer, Marianne Williamson, and Mike Dooley, in order to recognize how everything we put out in the world impacts our own journey. Nothing we do is isolated, and we are all connected. My sense is that we need to start caring about our brothers and sisters in the world a little bit more. This is the beginning of advocacy.

On Not Caring Enough

When we were children, we craved the days when we would be grown-ups. Our young minds pictured freedom and independence. We had this idea that as adults, we would be free to go wherever our whims led us during the rest of our days. That dream is both true and false. Bills, stress, limitations, fear, insecurity, and disbelief can alter the path. We wind up deflated and far away from that vision we had of ourselves. My hope is that through letter writing, we can slowly pare down and get back to that sense of excitement we valued about adult living. We must do this in order to prepare the upcoming generations to live an uplifted life full of possibilities. It's not a choice, people. It's our responsibility.

The adult collective has incredible power when it pertains to shaping the mind of a child. Yet, I can't figure out why we don't see this as a critical function of our individual lives. I believe that with pure intention and integrity, adults should be helping to inspire every child in their community. Imagine the magnitude of our impact. I can't quite understand why we permit unhappy, angry, burnt out, dissatisfied, yet power-wielding adults to implement the essential job of building the mind and character of our children. We owe it to each child on the planet to use our adult power with grace, humility, and respect.

Especially if our role is titled, TEACHER.

Dear Teachers and Other School Adults who refused to understand and help my child,

Shame on YOU!

Have you been so burnt out by the system that you are not willing to do everything possible to reach a child? I see you. I see how you talk about my son behind his back and humiliate him in front of his peers. It was easier to categorize him as bad, put him in the principals' office, and write him off. When in fact you, should have been responding to my requests to do whatever it took to help him succeed. There were SO many options, but you chose the easiest path, which was to stereotype him and cast him aside.

Shame on you.

I realize that some of you have your own issues, including a lack of dignity for the important work you do as teachers, yet you chose not to work as partners with our family. Maybe you should be honest with yourself and change careers. It felt like you weren't truly committed to helping my child succeed. It was simply more important for him to conform to your rules. Trust me, he tried. He needed much more compassion and care than simply following orders.

You made it a privilege for my son to go see the adult assigned to him for support. When he couldn't earn it, he would spend the rest of the day feeling unsafe. It was actually so simple, to let this other caring adult help him when he was befuddled by confusion. Instead, he was made to stew in his chaos. You took recess from him repeatedly because of his brain's impulse issues, and therefore, the one thing that would have helped calm his nervous system he was not allowed to have. You gave him candy for rewards and then sat him in time out for his body's angry response to the sugar. You humiliated him in front of his peers by calling him out, instead of taking him quietly to the side and speaking with him privately. You rarely worked with me, although I was willing to supply positive behavior charts, rewards, and even volunteer in the classroom to help you out.

You would say that you understood and were willing to work with me, but then my son would come home with reports of being screamed at, and I would see that your word was garbage. You refused to see that his neurological differences were real and required alternative solutions. He was an outcast and made to feel like a failure during the first 11 years of his life. Are you proud?

I don't want to forget the one adult who cornered me in the hallway with a worried look on her face sharing, "Mrs. Wolff you don't understand, I'm afraid that one day I'll see him in front of a judge." WHAT?!? Number one: don't put your fears on me ever. Number two: you only know the part of my child that cannot conform to groups. Try hearing me when I talk about how he needs a different learning environment, and his constant battle with the school stimulation causes him to feel like he is in a war zone. Listen to me when I share the strategies that work well with him. The two amazing skills he had were: a) he adored adults, so if he felt like you were on his team, he would do anything for you, and b) he could forgive easily. Why you didn't use those to his advantage, I'll never know.

Children have an abundance of skills and talents. At some point, we need to reframe the academic dialogue to assist children with uncovering those talents. At 8-years-old, my child was deemed an academic disaster. Yet he can fix just about anything. How many of the "brightest and the best" students can fix anything? How many of us wish we could?

Well, that was a long time ago, but I'm still super pissed about it. I want the world to know that my boy has moved mountains to create great things in his world. He is now 14 years old and this "failure" is operating a profitable car detailing, entrepreneurial business. Once a week, he unpacks groceries for a 97-year-old homebound woman. He is in a new school district with adults who go above and beyond the rules to help him succeed. It would have been a real blessing if he could have gotten to this point without all of the heartache caused by the fact that he is still a slow reader, and has difficulty in groups of children.

Wish we could have prevented many years of tears. It's all learning, right?

Oh well.
Wendy

On Nonsense

I'm hesitant to publish this letter. I can hear the backlash already. With the commitment to honesty, it remains included. Plus, I can hear my sister's voice telling me to not be such a chicken.

There are so many ridiculous trends that indicate I am old. Texting single letters to replace full words drives me insane. Spending days on end with video games instead of playing outside with a group of friends seems bizarre. Am I old or annoyed?

Dear Young Men who sag their pants,

PULL UP YOUR PANTS.

A belt is not meant for your knees. What kind of fashion is this? What is it about wearing your pants around your thighs with your ass crack visible to the world? Does it feel good? Is it a status thing? What happens when you need to run? Do you waddle? How do you purchase your jeans? Do you get pants that are one size bigger and a teeny, tiny belt that can be secured around the upper knee region? Do you have to go to a children's clothing store for a toddler belt? I realize I'm old, but I really am having trouble understanding this one.

I think you'd do much better in life if your pants were on your hips, with a belt properly securing them, and your shirt tucked in. Next time you are at 7-11, glance at a GQ magazine. You'll see that men can wear their pants on their hips and look fabulous.

Love,
Wendy

On Boredom

Developmentally, the teen brain is fascinating. It is ripe for learning new concepts. The energy level that comes with youth is something we all wish we had. Most of us believe that if we knew then what we know now, our lives as teenagers would have been much more fulfilling. Teen boredom needs to be fixed. This group with their skills, talents, and vigor can do anything, yet they don't. Teenagers have the ability to dream. They have incredible purchasing power. Couple this with their genuine skills and talents, and boredom could become a thing of the past. We must rapidly change this phenomenon. Why waste precious time sitting at home, texting, when they could be out there doing something grand?

Dear Teens,

I know! I know! There is NOTHING for you to do. It's time we really put an end to this ridiculous pattern. You kids are full of energy, creativity, excitement, adventure, and ability, yet we adults just leave you to your own devices to waste your precious days. As a collective, how can you change this?

We need a teenage revolution to get excited about the AMAZING attributes of the young people. I want to see you walking through the world using your skills and talents now. I want to see you developing new ideas, acting like entrepreneurs, creating exciting programs, and living life to the fullest. Instead of spending your days with your eyes glued to your phone screen, waiting for something to happen to you.

Get out and see what the world has to offer. Develop a ride share program so your fellow teens have a way to get places, and create new projects together. YOU are the future of this great country and the time is NOW. It's up to each and every one of us to make this world a better place. The world is WAITING for your contribution. Get to it!

Willing to help,
Wendy

On Snitching

Being called a snitch is possibly one of the worst names to be associated with as a kid. This might be one of the most dangerous social concepts of our era. Everyone deserves to have the onslaught of physical and/or mental abuse coming at him or her to stop immediately. What a disastrous concept; stay quiet, allow the cruelty to continue, because the other option of getting help will create an even harsher uproar. Holy %$#*!

This is one social norm that needs a rapid adjustment.

> Dear Whomever made up the norm about snitching,
>
> Are you kidding?
>
> Answer this. When a child needs the help of an adult and is afraid for fear of the retribution associated with snitching, what is there to do? If you think this isn't an issue, ask any kid if they want to be known as a snitch. Ask them how they get help when they are being bullied at school. Ask them if adults can help them when someone is harassing them.
>
> I do ask. And the answer is almost always, I am afraid of the revenge that will come at me for

telling. WHAT?!?! Are you freaking kidding me? So, what I'm hearing you say is you can't get help because it will only get worse if you tell? Is that right? Can't we do better than this for our children?

If anything needs to change in the world, this needs to be one of the first things. Everyone deserves to be able to get help. Everyone deserves to feel safe and not be hurt.

And we wonder why the bullying problem keeps getting worse.

Not interested in standing by and letting violence continue,

Wendy

On Raising Good People

As a parent, there is nothing more important than raising good, kind children. It also isn't a guessing game. Kids need involved, engaging parents that guide them as their brain and character develops. If I had a dime for every inappropriate comment, phrase, or picture posted on my kid's social media sites from their classmates, I'd be rich! Why we think that it's acceptable to let kids have unregulated access to the immense cyber world is beyond me. Let's bring back outdoor play, modesty, and human interaction in real time.

Dear Parents of today and tomorrow,

Guess what? When you bought your child that new smart phone and decided that you don't need to regularly check what they are doing on it, you made a distinct decision to pay for and provide unlimited access to a private world that allows your child to experience violence, sex, hatred, and negativity, without monitoring any of it. Why would you do this?

Years back, a friend of mine that raised three successful teens, told me one of his greatest parenting tips: NO such thing as privacy for a child/teen. He used to listen to voicemails, read through instant messages (back then there was limited texting), and communicate with his kids about what he found. I took it to heart, and through the years of raising my own children, saw how I was setting myself up to fail (as well as them) when I allowed them to sit with their devices and privately mastermind chaos.

We have to come together and find a way to raise good, kind, sensitive kids, who understand that contributing to the greater good in the world is the best thing they can do for their development and for humanity. We have to show adolescents that there is value in being an upstanding community member in this world. We need to help them identify their gifts and talents early on in life, and NOT WAIT for society or school to dictate what is absolutely fascinating about our children. Only then will we be able to finally change the downward societal spiral. At that point, we will be able to impact teen bullying, violence, and suicide. At a very basic, grassroots level, each one of us needs to value, honor, respect, and assist all of the children in every community to grow up to be amazing contributors in the world. It starts with me. It starts with you.

Hurry up,
Wendy

On Providing Help

Violence is disturbing. When brutality is inflicted upon another human being, there is an indication that something is clearly wrong. The equipment that caused the viciousness is only part of the cause, and not nearly the complete solution. Thankfully, within the past two years, the dialogue is now forming to discuss the lack of mental health services for people in distress. My feeling is that we are WAY TOO LATE. Quick, decisive action to provide low-cost therapeutic services for families and individuals is imperative. The writing is already on the wall, people. All that is left to do is ACT.

Dear Mental Health Experts,

How is the lack of affordable mental health care in the United States not one of our primary issues being addressed? Maybe I'm not clued in, but it seems that every time there is a massive gun-related tragedy, the only thing that is discussed is gun control. While I am ALL IN FAVOR of limiting access to weapons, which kill our citizens of the world, I am SHOCKED that the discussion only gets this far.

Doesn't the world know that if someone has the ability to pick up a gun and kill another being, there is something going on in their mind that is the root cause of that violent act? Doesn't it seem smarter to spend money helping people to heal, rather than waiting for the next time someone storms a school and annihilates everyone that crosses their path?

Is anyone discussing some of the very serious mental health issues that cause individuals to be completely disconnected from other human beings? Do you know that there are thousands of parents out there in the world that have no way to get help for their children who are exhibiting severe anti-social, anti-attachment behaviors? Can you believe that many of them have NO financial means to seek what limited help exists, so they remain alone in their battle to help prevent a major catastrophe from occurring because their child's mental health status was never treated?

So many questions. SO LITTLE TIME. You're the experts, do something! This is me doing something.

Respectfully,

Wendy Wolff, MPH

Chapter Seven –

To You

Thank you. I am grateful that you spent your hard-earned money to buy this book. I hope my words and personal experiences inspired you to create a more positive experience in your own life. Connect with me at www.wendywolff.com and share your magnificence.

Together, we can make great things happen.

On Next Steps

My list of letters to write is long. The first iteration of The Letter Writing Project had a plan to include every single letter. I soon realized that it was not possible or practical. My own personal next step is to buy myself some nice stationary and get the rest of these letters out of my heart and into the universe for healing.

Dear Family & Friends,

Through helping myself to heal, I am hoping to create love among sisters, brothers, friends, neighbors, and family members.

I lamented about how some of you would feel left out when bits and pieces of a story got told and didn't include you. The painstaking process of eliminating letters from this book was not easy, and led me to be afraid of your disapproval. It halted my process for months. Then, I realized this was almost a good problem to have. Too many letters to write. How fortunate!

Had I truly written to everyone of influence, the pages would have exceeded a practical limit. Be assured that two of the absolutely most important people in my life, my sons, were purposefully excluded. Their letters have been gathered since they were little boys and will be presented to them one day in a very private way.

As I have recommended to the reader, I too will be writing my own letters and placing them in the mail. While your letter was not ultimately published, it exists deep inside my ever grateful heart.

Your letters are coming. I cannot wait to write them!

Love,
Wendy

On Writing Letters

During the editing process, I heard from a woman, who after seeing a Facebook post about *The Letter Writing Project*, decided to change her entire life. Her typical response when social interactions got her angry was to immediately fire off a furious letter to the antagonist. She would often isolate herself from the world as she stewed in a gruesome rage. One day, after reading about my work, she reached out. She shared that The Letter Writing Project inspired her to write a letter with possibilities for a happier outcome, rather than a venomous stream of accusations. She felt herself release negativity and embrace a new way to love. Could I ask for anything more?

Dear Reader,

Thank you so much for reading *The Letter Writing Project*. This is your chance to figure out what lies deep inside of you. What do you care about? What pisses you off? What can you help to change? Who do you love? Do they know it? Who changed your life? Do you know the top five people who contributed to the amazing person you are today? Have they ever been thanked? The only goal is to help us make the world a brighter, kinder place. We can get to know ourselves better, and develop the lives we deserve, by creating our own honest perspective through the art of letter writing. It can be something we all share.

I am deeply grateful that you used your valuable time to read the words that were in my heart. To help you engage in your own letter writing process, there are a few simple rules and steps to take. First, you can always contact me directly at www.wendywolff.com, and schedule a workshop for your friends. We can do this simply through technology, or in person. Either way works. Second, you can drop me a line and let me know how this book helped you to free yourself from burden.

Below are some suggested guidelines for getting the most rewarding experience from your letter writing craft.

- Mail only the letters that you are proud of and that will make the world a better place. Only send something that will lift a person up in their life. The Letter Writing Project firmly believes that only good should come of your letters.

- Never, ever mail something that will harm anyone. If you need to write that nasty letter because you are furious, go ahead and write it. However, never, ever mail this type of letter. Unkind letters do no one any good, even if you have been seriously wronged. I have no intention of ever connecting with the man whose car killed Donna, but it sure felt AMAZING to get in touch with how insanely furious I am about it. You can always write it and shred it into tiny pieces to get it out of your system.

- The Letter Writing Project was designed as a step towards healing and living a life of joy and peace. We don't always need the other person to hear us in order to release our pain or anger. Oftentimes, simply acknowledging that we hold pain, and then using the art of letter writing to let those emotions seep out onto the paper, is enough to start the healing process. These letters are to release the feelings that have been constricting you. In my personal life, if this still does not provide any relief, then I get additional support from either a caring friend or a professional. I was taught this by Donna many moons ago.

Along with the rules, I have some other tips to help you gain the most out of your letter writing experience.

- **Music** — Listening to music can evoke a range of emotions, helping you to connect with your true feelings. Find that special piece of music, or the artist that you love to play in the background during your writing session. Discover songs that remind you of the person that you are addressing. I found that Dave Matthew's song, Sister, about his own sister's death, was incredibly helpful for me to sob with. Music will help spark your creativity. Let it lead you to cry, laugh, scream, growl, and retreat.

- **Quiet** — As this is an intensely personal

process, it is a good idea to write your letters in a space where you can think. Writing at the kitchen table while the kids are doing their homework is probably going to be distracting. They might even wonder why you are crying. I prefer a quiet space with my favorite notebook. Sometimes I write in a coffee shop, sometimes on my back patio. It really depends on the day, but always, it is when I am alone.

- **Writing Materials** — I love writing implements. Mostly I love a good pencil, but there are some pens that I adore. Pick out a pen or pencil that is your favorite. Get yourself a good notebook that speaks to you. Since 1997, my choice of journal has been a black and white composition notebook; however, there are hundreds to choose from.

- **Settings** — You can write just about anywhere – as long as you have paper and something to make the marks on your page. Treat yourself to an hour with a steaming hot cup of coffee at the local café. Lose yourself in the world of your thoughts amidst the other writers, readers, and customers around you. Find a park bench overlooking a beautiful creek. Sit under a sprawling tree. Puff up your pillows, put on some special lighting, and sit in bed. Anywhere works that provides you with a distraction-free experience.

- **Hydrate** — Sipping on a glass of water while you craft your letters provides an opportunity to be still. The motion of putting the pen down, picking up the glass, drinking, and being nourished, helps to harness your energy and quiet your mind. Being still for this moment allows you to keep that energy at a nice, calm level to continue an attempt at unveiling your honest self.

- **Pride** — Be incredibly proud of yourself. Participating in the Letter Writing Movement is a gift that you are giving to yourself. It's a chance for you to clear. Allow yourself to smile, have a laugh, hug or pat your own back for the accomplishment. This is a fabulous step towards living a balanced life. When we clear ourselves of the negative emotions that are binding us, and experience pure love for others, we carve a path to our own personal success. Feel your FREEDOM expand!

- **Waiting** — I like to draft a letter and then wait. Step away for at least an hour to let the emotional self settle down. This is especially true when you are writing words that may come out of sadness, anger, or grief. When I go back to re-read, I typically end up either crying or laughing. I feel so satisfied with my accomplishment that sometimes I even jump up and dance. Remember, if the letter will invoke negativity for another person, even while you are feeling less burdened, DO NOT send it.

- **Keep a Copy** — One of the greatest women of all time, my college roommate, taught me the trick of saving all of your letters. Not the ones that you receive (although that is always lovely), but the ones that you compose.

About 20 years ago, while we were both broke graduate students living hand-to-mouth in NYC, she shared with me the volumes of letters she had photocopied and kept in a binder. The gleaming expression in her eyes was so monumental, and since that day, I have been writing letters and attempting to keep a set for myself. I'm not always the best at it, but the gift of reading them is astounding. Try and be diligent with this. You'll love the reward. As the years wear on, it will become even more meaningful to be reminded of how you expressed yourself. The book of email exchanges between Donna and I is another example of the benefit of saving your letters.

- **Join the letter writing movement** — Share your experience with me and the rest of the letter writers via Facebook, Twitter, or www.wendywolff.com I would love to have you be part of the process of healing our hearts and minds. Let's make the world a better place together.

Love,
Wendy

Chapter Eight –
The Final Conversation

The final letter in this series is the one that I actually started with. I have edited this letter, which was read at her memorial service, to protect the privacy of anyone that needs it. If you were there, then you heard this before. If you were not, know that this was the hardest and most meaningful assignment I had ever been given.

On Being Sisters

Dear Donna,

Talk about the impossible. There have been days that I hung up the phone after my 4th call with mom thinking, "Mom is getting older and someday I may not have the luxury of talking with her." I would do this often to prepare myself, because talking to mom was almost as regular as breathing. But something I never, ever imagined was a day without you.

In daily life, I often stop and think to myself – today is a good day. This moment is lovely, and I relish in it. But since it never entered my mind that there would be a world without you in it, I was not prepared. Forty-six years of silently knowing each other was there, even if we lived far apart or were too busy to connect. There was a Donna and there was Donna's little sister.

There was never a time in my life that you weren't peering over my shoulder, making sure my life was on track. When I didn't come home from my friend's house that time Mom went to China, you gave me fifteen minutes to walk two miles and get myself home, or else, and I did it. When I graduated from college, and had the worst year of my life, seeing things in the adult world for the first time, you got me out of a downhill spiral that helped me slowly to move on up to who I am today.

And when I called you to say that I would never meet a man who was kind and stable, handsome and funny, you said... you are looking in the wrong place. Look for the good guy. Sure enough, weeks later, Marc appeared. I know how much you loved Marc. It was easy to see, because the moments we had together, I quickly became the butt of the joke, the outsider... which meant he was in.

Here is a list of some things that only you and I loved together:

- We loved when our baby cousins were born and we finally had living dolls to play with.

- We loved me poking you consistently and you slapping my hand away, laughing.

- We loved playing practical tricks on mom, even as recent as when we were hiding around the corner, outside of the restaurant, and watching her wander around looking for us.

- We loved the feeling that we both shared when we held hands.

- We loved a good visit with each other in which we would share our new favorite jewelry, and then inevitably trade a ring or two.

- We loved buying each other a matching coffee cup or little dish, so that when we both looked at it, we knew that the other was there.

- We loved shoving our arms in each other's lap and demanding TICKLE.
- We loved the joy that our sons would get when Uncle would show up. Even if he was TOO LOUD.
- We loved dreaming about skiing together and then actually skiing together.
- We loved a good salt bagel, no cream cheese, please.
- We loved our matching dresses, culottes, and Danskin outfits, that Grandma would make us wear.
- We loved playing cards for hours with Grandma and Grandpa, which of course, would always end in a laughing fit.
- We loved sticking our cold feet under each other while sharing a cup of coffee. Or maybe I just loved that.
- We loved our dogs.
- We loved when your youngest son would crawl with a book into a lap and remain there, requiring repeat reading of the same story over and over.
- We loved when your oldest son would say his complete, full name at 3-years-old, when people would ask him what his name was.
- We loved when my baby would interrupt little rabbit fufu with, "it's naughty, it's naughty,

it's naughty."

- We loved when my oldest son would laugh at a joke and sparkles would shoot out of his eyes.

- We loved when our only niece would act as the ultimate leader of her baby boy cousins, and spend a perfectly equal amount of time with each. How we marveled at that.

- And our favorite thing that we loved was the long walk you would take with two babies, just to meet me at the airport, so we could watch them run as fast as they could into my arms.

I am luckier than others, Don, because my hands LOOK like yours. I feel like you in my mannerisms when I am speaking to my children, or going throughout my day. Before April 2nd, it was merely an observation; today it becomes a gift.

I will miss everything about you. I will miss seeing your number pop up, and knowing that the first words out of your mouth will be, "Hi Wen," and mine will be, "Hi Don". I will miss snorting and cackling about the silliest things. I will even miss your constant questioning to make sure, as always, that I was making the proper choices and on the right track. You should know that I am.

I promise that I will take care of mom, so you don't have to worry about that. We always worried about her together. So today, I will take that on, happily. Your text to me last year during her near death scare made me certain that you knew – that with me around, mom will always be just fine.

Forever and a day, you were craving for a way to contribute to making the world a place that fit your vision. Ever since I can remember, you had this unsettling feeling that kept you searching. And it wasn't until you met and married your husband that you made strides towards finding your purpose. Seeing all these faces of all of the lives that you graced with your kindness and perseverance showed me that you made it. And that is worth celebrating, sister.

Finally, (and sorry it took me so long to get here), you and I loved so much the way my baby said, "I love you," that I will say it once more today... in your honor: "Aluhbue."

Love, Wen

Our last words between two sisters the day she was killed. Mine never were received.

About the Author

Wendy Wolff spends most of her days working with others to make their lives easier. Over the past twenty years she has positively impacted communities throughout the United States with her work as a strategic planning consultant. Wendy's forte is to recognize the issues that impede the ability to thrive and develop appropriate solutions that lead to an improved quality of life. Her collection of essays aimed at making life easier can be found in several magazines including Kidz Edge Magazine, The Indypendent Reader, and Your Teen Magazine. After the tragic loss of her sister in a car accident, she started the idea for the Letter Writing Project, and her goal is to get the world around her writing letters again – for the purpose of healing and dealing with the joys and tragedies of life.

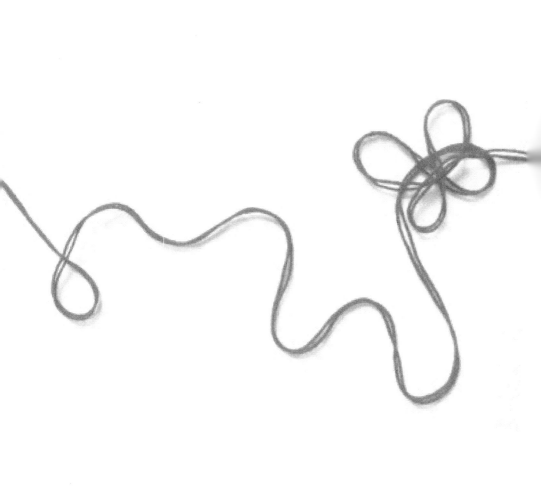